# HIDING
## TO
# SURVIVE

# HIDING
# TO
# SURVIVE

STORIES OF
JEWISH CHILDREN RESCUED
FROM THE HOLOCAUST

## MAXINE B. ROSENBERG

CLARION BOOKS
NEW YORK

Clarion Books
a Houghton Mifflin Company imprint
215 Park Avenue South, New York, NY 10003
Copyright © 1994 by Maxine B. Rosenberg

Text is 12.25 point Times.
Book design by Sylvia Frezzolini

Printed in the U.S.A.

Library of Congress Cataloging-in-Publication Data
Rosenberg, Maxine B.
Hiding to survive: stories of Jewish children rescued from the
Holocaust / Maxine Rosenberg.    p.    cm.
Summary: First person accounts of fourteen Holocaust survivors who
as children were hidden from the Nazis by non-Jews.
ISBN: 0-395-65014-3    PA ISBN: 0-395-90020-4
1. Holocaust, Jewish (1939–1945)—Personal narratives—Juvenile literature.
2. Jewish children—Biography—Juvenile literature.    3. World War, 1939-1945—
Children—Juvenile literature.    4. Righteous Gentiles in the Holocaust—Juvenile
literature.    5. Holocaust survivors—Biography—Juvenile literature.
[1. Holocaust, Jewish (1939–1945)—
Personal narratives.    2. Holocaust survivors.
3. Righteous Gentiles in the Holocaust. 4. Jews—Biography.] I. Title.
D804.3.R6625    1994
940.53'18'0922—dc20
[B]                                        93-28328
CIP
AC
Rev.

HOR  10 9 8 7 6 5 4

To Dorothy Briley—

*for being there from the very beginning*

# CONTENTS

| | |
|---|---|
| INTRODUCTION | 1 |
| Paulette Pomeranz | 11 |
| Kurt Dattner | 19 |
| Rose Silberberg-Skier | 29 |
| Manny Stern | 43 |
| Cécile Rojer Jeruchim | 53 |
| Jacques van Dam | 63 |
| Sylvia Richter | 73 |
| Andy Sterling | 85 |
| Hirsch Grunstein | 95 |
| Aviva Blumberg | 107 |
| Ruth Bachner | 117 |
| Debora Biron | 129 |
| Simon Jeruchim | 139 |
| Judith Steel | 151 |
| ACKNOWLEDGMENTS | 161 |
| GLOSSARY | 162 |
| FURTHER READING | 165 |

# HIDING
## TO
# SURVIVE

# Introduction

On January 30, 1933, Adolf Hitler became chancellor of Germany. Under his dictatorship a reign of terror prevailed throughout most of Europe. More savagery and violence took place during the next twelve years than in any thousand-year period in history. Countries were invaded, and people of all nationalities were brutally murdered. But no group was persecuted as much as the Jews. With Hitler as its leader, the Nazi party sent six million Jews to their death.

When Hitler came to power, his plan to annihilate the Jews was no secret. Eight years earlier, in his book, *Mein Kampf (My Struggle)*, Hitler had described the Jews as Germany's greatest enemy and said they had to be eliminated. Also, as leader and main speaker of the Nazi (National Socialist German Workers) party, Hitler told vicious lies about the Jews. He said that by Jews intermarrying with Germans—the master race—German blood was being poisoned.

Other groups such as homosexuals, the disabled, and inhabitants of Slavic countries were also harmful to Germany, Hitler said, but none were as dangerous as the Jews.

1

In 1920, when Hitler assumed command of the Nazi party, it consisted of a small band of ruthless individuals whom few took seriously. But little by little the party grew as more people in Germany became unhappy. The country had just lost World War I, German money wasn't worth much, and many people had no jobs.

Hitler gave them hope. He promised that if the Nazi party came into power, young and old, rich and poor would have a better life. He also vowed that one day Germany would become a great force and rule the world. But first the Jews had to be annihilated, he said. They were the cause of all of Germany's problems.

Meanwhile, conditions in Germany kept worsening. By 1929 unemployment had reached an all-time high, and people didn't know where to turn for help. Instead of trying to understand why their country was in trouble, they accepted Hitler's lies and blamed everything on the Jews. Soon doctors, teachers, and businessmen were joining the Nazi party. When Hitler came to power in 1933, his following had grown considerably.

Now as chancellor Hitler could put his ideas into action. Immediately freedom of speech was abolished and political enemies of the Nazi party were killed. The SS, a black-shirted security guard, and the Gestapo, a special police force, were established, making door-to-door arrests and randomly attacking Jews on the street.

Everywhere, on radios that blasted day and night in offices, cafes, and homes, people heard the same hateful messages: "Jews are filthy. Jews are greedy. Jews drink blood of Christian children." In the movies, in newspapers, on posters, and in schools, verbal attacks were made against

2

Jews. German children were even given permission to spit on them.

Jews now could not go to restaurants, theaters, or swimming pools. Their stores were boycotted, and mobs who looted the stores went unpunished.

The Jews were in shock. They had been living in Germany for centuries and had been accepted in German society. Jewish men had helped Germany fight in the wars. Many Jews who weren't religious had thought of themselves first as Germans. Now the Nazis were saying that Jews were impure and had to be gotten rid of.

The Jews were terrified. They didn't know whom to trust. Christian and Jewish friends became suspicious of one another. Everyone lived in fear.

Some Jews managed to leave Germany, although travel was no longer permitted. They went to other European countries that they thought were safer. Those with enough money and the right connections sailed to America or to Palestine (now Israel).

Most Jews, though, stayed in Germany. They were sure that the German people would rise against Hitler and that the outside world would soon take action.

But the outside world just waited and watched as the SS and Gestapo rounded up by the thousands people they claimed were "traitors." At the same time, German children were encouraged to spy on their parents and to report to the authorities anyone who expressed disagreement with Nazi activities. Those Germans who opposed Hitler were too frightened to make a move.

Each day the Jews lost more rights. They were no longer considered German citizens. They were forbidden to work.

Jewish children could not go to school. Jews from Eastern European countries who had held jobs in Germany were shipped back home, while others were hauled away to slave labor camps.

Germans who had been unemployed were given the jobs that Jews once held, and more jobs were created by the government as it began to prepare for war with neighboring countries. Most of the German people thanked Hitler for improving their lives.

On March 12, 1938, German troops invaded Austria. Immediately Hitler started rounding up Jews in that country too. Eight months later, on the nights of November 9 and 10, hundreds of synagogues and thousands of Jewish homes and shops in Germany and Austria were destroyed. Jews trying to escape were shot, and twenty thousand Jews were arrested. It was the most gruesome act toward Jews since Hitler had taken control. Later in history this cruel event became known as *Kristallnacht,* Night of the Broken Glass, because of all the windows that were smashed.

The following March German troops overran Czechoslovakia, and that September they invaded Poland. At this point England and France, who had a treaty with Poland, came to defend the country, and World War II was declared.

Within a month Poland was defeated. It had the largest population of Jews in Europe. Once again the Nazis tormented these people. Tens of thousands were forced to move into ghettos in the slum sections of the city. The largest ghetto was in Warsaw.

The next spring Germany invaded Denmark, Holland, Belgium, and France. Jews all over Europe frantically fled from one country to the next trying to find a safe place, but

4

the Nazis were everywhere. In the end most of Europe's Jews were trapped.

By 1942 Hitler's final plan to eliminate the Jews was in full force. Every day thousands of Jews were shipped from the ghettos to concentration camps where they were put to death.

Jewish parents had to make a major decision, to stay together as a family and risk being killed, or to try and find a non-Jewish person, usually a stranger, who would hide their child. Most parents who decided to hand their child over to a Gentile waited until the last minute.

The number of Jewish children who were hidden during the Holocaust is estimated to be somewhere between ten thousand and five hundred thousand. The range is so vast because there are no records of the children and rescuers who were caught and killed by the Nazis. Nor is it known how many children survived by hiding but have preferred to keep their story private.

In any case, it's guessed that about 1 percent of the Gentile population in Europe hid Jewish children. Although this number was small, the courage of these rescuers was tremendous. Children were lucky to be placed with these Gentiles, but they still had to live through the war.

Many of those children who survived were hidden in monasteries and convents. Because of their size and staff, these religious institutions could take in larger numbers than could individual families. More important, the individual priests and nuns were willing to take the risk of hiding Jewish children.

A lot of children were hidden on farms in remote areas, where it was thought the Nazis were less likely to come.

Others were in city apartment buildings and houses—behind closets, in attics, and in cellars. Some children were hidden in underground sewers with rats crawling alongside them.

No matter where they were, none of the children were totally safe. More often than not, they moved from one hiding place to another when the situation became too dangerous. Even those who remained with their original rescuers throughout the Holocaust lived in constant fear of being caught or denounced. And if they were separated from their parents, they always worried that they might never see them again.

Today these children are adults, most of them in their fifties and sixties. When they talk about their past, they can't believe they have survived such terror. Yet until recently few shared their experiences with family members or close friends. They thought no one would be interested in hearing about their sufferings. Also because they hadn't been sent to the concentration camps, they felt they had no right to complain. In addition, they didn't want to relive the painful memories of childhood. So they kept their early lives a secret.

Then an international conference for hidden children was held in New York City in May 1991. Sixteen hundred former hidden children, and some invited rescuers, came from all over the world to talk about their experiences during the war. They realized they were getting older, and if their stories weren't told now, future generations wouldn't know what had taken place.

At the conference it was discussed how in wartime, when lives are at stake, people often behave in unexpected ways. Hidden children told about Germans who helped Jews to escape and Jews who informed on one another. When it came to hiding Jewish children, it was also difficult to predict who would assist and who would refuse. Usually a person was approached by someone he knew and asked to make a spur-of-the-moment decision. Sometimes the least likely person would say yes. Peasants, housekeepers, teachers, and farmers who had been known to speak negatively about Jews agreed to take them in; intellectuals who detested Hitler's policy toward the Jews declined out of fear.

In most instances the children and their rescuers had never met before. What motivated the rescuers to help was the desire to save an innocent life and hatred of living under Nazi control.

In countries with a long history of anti-Semitism, it was particularly dangerous to hide Jews. Neighbors and the local police would denounce the rescuers and the Jews they were hiding and turn them over to the Nazis. Sometimes whole towns were burned as a punishment. In spite of this danger, numerous Gentiles in these countries still hid Jewish children. By saving a life, they changed history.

In 1953 the Israeli government passed a Martyrs' and Heroes' Remembrance Law that defined "high-minded Gentiles who risked their lives to save Jews" during the war. Plaques engraved with their names have been placed at Yad Vashem, the museum in Jerusalem that memorializes European Jews who died in the Holocaust and the Christians who attempted to save them. Also, the Anti-Defamation League sends monthly stipends to needy and elderly rescuers to make their lives easier.

Many of the rescuers in this book have been honored by Yad Vashem or by their own country. When some of them received their awards, they modestly said, "I only did what I'd hope another human being would do for me." That response was typical.

Although the rescuers may have come from everyday walks of life, they are the real heroes in history. Because of them, the children they hid are alive today and are able to share their stories.

*Paulette Pomeranz, age 13, in 1947.*

# PAULETTE POMERANZ

GREECE

*"Everything became a secret"*

When I was very young, my parents got divorced. My mother ran her own business, and she found it too hard to take care of me. Instead I went to live with Eli, one of her workers, and Eli's family. Their religion was Greek Orthodox, and they had a house ten minutes from Athens, the city where I was born and where my mother had her store.

For the next three years, while Eli's mother, Julia, watched me, my mother visited a lot, and my father and older brother, Daniel, who lived with him, came to see me too.

Then in 1941, when I was seven and a half, Greece was divided up between Germany and Italy. The Italians, who were in charge of Athens, pretty much left the Jews alone. But things were very dangerous in the German-occupied areas. In Salonika, where my relatives and most Greek Jews lived, Jews were being rounded up and taken away.

One night my mother came by and woke me. She said she was leaving to find a safer country for us and that she would soon return for me. I was so sleepy, I didn't know what she was talking about.

A few months later I heard shouting in the house. "The Germans are here! They're all over the place," Julia was screaming in panic. She had no idea where my mother was and didn't know what to do with me.

By then we had become very attached. After living with her for so long, I called her "Mama." On Sundays I went to church with her and her daughters. But I was still Jewish, and Julia was worried. The next morning she took me to a synagogue so we could talk to a rabbi.

It was the first time I had ever been inside a synagogue. Since my family didn't observe our religion or celebrate any of the holidays, I knew more about Greek Orthodoxy than I did about Judaism.

Julia told the rabbi that she had heard rumors about Germans rounding up Jews and asked whether she should have me baptized for safety. The rabbi said, "Do what you must to protect the child."

As soon as we got home, Julia gave me a cross and told me I had to wear it all the time. She also said that when I left the house I was always to stay with my friend Athena, who was five years older than I. Athena knew I was Jewish and was going to watch out for me.

Meanwhile Julia warned me not to give out any information about our lives. No one was to know we had visited the rabbi or what went on inside our house. Everything became a secret.

In 1943 the Italian government fell, and the Germans took over the rest of Greece. They set up headquarters in my school, across the street from our house. Every time I walked by, I was terrified. I was sure a German would grab me and take me away on a train.

The townspeople were frightened too. Although I was the only Jewish person in the neighborhood, they knew that if the Germans found out, we'd all be shot. Yet they did everything to help me. One day the baker told Julia that if I were ever in serious danger, I should go directly to his shop, and he'd show me an escape route he had mapped out.

Still, I could never relax. At night I kept my shoes and winter coat next to my bed in case of an emergency.

By then there were tremendous food shortages. Sometimes we had so little to eat, Julia would count out raisins for dinner. She'd hand me most of her portion and say, "I'm not hungry."

Usually, though, there was some rice, soup, vegetables, or bread. But other people in town weren't as lucky. I was afraid one of them might denounce me for a cup of flour or a tablespoon of sugar.

Meanwhile I got a letter from my mother telling me she was in America. She said that when the war was over, she'd send for me. Now I had no idea when I'd see her, or my father and Daniel, who were running from place to place trying to hide from the Germans.

At least I had Julia. She treated me like a princess. Whenever she'd get a piece of material, she'd sew me pretty clothes and tie ribbons in my hair. She also did everything to keep me safe. But I wasn't sure what she'd do if the situation got too dangerous.

I tried to please her to make sure she'd never send me away. I volunteered to wash the floors, make the beds, and run errands. When the Germans started taking all the bread from the bakery, I got up before dawn, slipped into the shop, and left with a small loaf the baker had given me hidden under my arm. I wanted Julia to see I was a good girl and that she needed me.

Now that the Germans occupied my school, I only went to makeshift classes twice a week in the church basement. The other days I played ball or hide-and-seek with my friends. Mostly we talked about food when we were together. When my friends asked what I wished I could eat at that very moment, I always said white bread, sugar, and chocolate.

Sometimes a neighbor would hear what was being sold on the black market and would tell Athena and me. We'd go to that person's house or meet on the corner to make a deal. I'd ask, ''How much do you want for a glass of oil?'' and the person would say, ''How about a carton of cigarettes?'' More often I had money or a tiny piece of gold that Julia had given me, and I'd trade with that. I was good at this job, and that pleased Julia.

One night there was loud knocking on the door. When Julia looked out the window, she saw two Gestapo officers, each with a barking German shepherd on a leash. ''Get under the covers and pretend you're asleep,'' she told me.

The German officers said they had found a parachute and were looking for the British paratrooper who owned it. Julia said she knew nothing about this and offered them coffee. As they sat around the table, they showed her pictures of their families.

In 1944 the Allies started bombing Athens. Whenever the sirens sounded, everybody ran for shelter to an open trench in the town square. Our only protection was cooking pots we wore on our heads. My helmet was a frying pan that I kept under my bed. I tried to make a game of the whole thing, but I was always scared. I never knew if I'd reach the trench in time.

All the while Julia kept trying to give me hope. She'd

14

describe how wonderful America was and tell me that one day I'd live there and have everything I could want. Although I didn't want to leave Julia, the fantasy of becoming an actress and being rich appealed to me. I'd have enough money to send Julia a nice warm coat for the winter.

Meanwhile my life was very difficult. My shoes had worn out, and the soles flopped when I walked. My coat too was threadbare, so Julia put newspapers inside my clothing to keep me warm. "Just wait till you get to America," she kept saying. But sometimes I wasn't sure I would last long enough to make it there.

Then one day I overheard Julia tell her daughters that all of my relatives in Salonika had perished. By this same time my father and Daniel had stopped visiting. I was frightened that something bad must have happened to them too.

To make things worse, the bombing increased and lots of British planes were being shot down. In the morning my friends and I would see white parachutes lying in the street and race out to grab them before they were found by the Germans. As Julia cut and sewed the parachutes to make sheets and dresses for me, the two of us would try to figure out who was hiding the men. If we saw someone buying extra food, we'd suspect that family. Naturally we kept this a secret too.

Suddenly, one summer morning in 1945, I woke up and noticed that the Germans had vacated my school. They must have left in the night. Whatever, it was the last I ever saw of them. The next thing I knew, English tanks were on the road, and the soldiers were throwing chocolates and caramels to everyone. It was the first time since the war had begun that people acted happy.

15

A few months later I got a letter from my mother, saying she was trying to get papers for me to come to America. After that she sent a package through the Red Cross. It contained a skirt, a jacket, shoes, a sweater, and a volley-ball. Now I was the queen of the neighborhood.

Six to eight months later my mother wrote again, this time to say she was coming to Greece to take me back with her to America. Also, my father and Daniel visited me. Daniel, who was nineteen, was leaving for Palestine, where many Jewish children were settling. He and my father wanted to know if I'd like to go too, but Julia said no.

Then one day my mother arrived, and Julia and I went to the boat to meet her. I recognized her from the photos Julia had shown me over the years, but when she kissed me hello, I felt I was greeting a stranger.

It took some months before my mother could get me a ticket to America. Finally, in January 1947, everything was ready. I was then thirteen years old.

"I'll send you clothes and food from America," I told Julia and my friends as they hugged me good-bye. They were all crying, but I felt nothing. I was like a robot.

For the next year in America I refused to unpack my suitcase. I was determined to go back to Greece and wrote to Julia and my friends telling them how lonely I was. At Eastertime Julia sent me a tin of my favorite cookies, which made me miss her even more.

In the meantime my mother remarried, and within a few years she had two more children. We kids became close, but I still kept thinking about Julia and my friends in Greece. Finally, in 1958, my mother said Julia could come visit us, and she helped pay the fare.

16

Julia liked America so much, she decided to stay, and soon her daughters joined her. After that I had my two mothers in America and my Greek family nearby.

*Paulette in 1993.*

POSTSCRIPT

Until she died a few months ago at age ninety-three, Julia and I lived near each other. I visited her a couple of times a week, and I continued to call her "Mama." My children called her "Yaya," which is Greek for *grandmother*.

My family celebrated the Greek holidays with her, and when I started observing Jewish holidays, she and her family were at our Passover table.

I was with Julia to the end of her life. She was my other mother. She gave me a home and affection and kept me safe. I could never repay her for what she had done.

*Paulette owns a number of businesses.*

17

*Kurt Dattner, age 14, and his mother with Peper and Titine Phillipp.* (Credit: Museum of Jewish Heritage, New York)

# KURT DATTNER

## *"I kept thinking about those times I had almost been caught by the Gestapo"*

I was born in Aachen, Germany, and lived with my parents in an apartment across the street from my grandparents' house. I was especially close to my grandfather and constantly with him. He spoiled me.

Although my family was Jewish, we weren't at all religious. We didn't even celebrate Chanukah. Yet the Germans wouldn't let my father, a concert pianist, perform in public because he was a Jew.

In 1938, when I was five, the Germans began vandalizing synagogues and destroying shops owned by Jews. My grandparents had already left for China, but my father couldn't get the right papers, so we stayed in Germany for another year and then escaped to Belgium. In 1940 the Germans invaded that country.

At first they didn't bother the Jews much, but by mid-1941 we had to wear a star on our clothing. And when I went to the movies, they kept showing the same short film of long-bearded, dirty Jewish men who had rats crawling around them. Now I could count on Belgian children beating me up on my way to and from school.

Each day the situation got worse, until finally my parents

decided to send me to a Catholic orphanage where they thought I'd be safer. When they told me this, I cried.

Before my father took me to the orphanage, he explained that I'd have to go to church there two or three times a day. "The nuns and the priest know you are Jewish and want to protect you," he said. "You must follow what they tell you to do. But that doesn't mean you have to believe their religion." I was very confused.

The first thing the nuns did was cut off my hair so I wouldn't get lice. Then they gave me baptism lessons. On the day I was converted, my name was changed to Jean Pierre DeClere, and I was given Christian godparents who knew I was Jewish.

My parents visited now and then, and every time they left, I hated saying good-bye. I was lonely in the orphanage, and the food was terrible. Except for the package of bread with onions and butter that my mother sent and an occasional sandwich a teacher would slip me, I was always hungry. Once when I visited my godparents' friend, I ate everything that was green in her garden.

At the orphanage there were two other children whose parents were alive, and I suspected from their sad eyes and worried faces that they too must be Jewish. Still, I couldn't imagine they were as miserable as I. During classes I could barely concentrate on my work because I was thinking so much about food and my parents. By then my mother and father were no longer visiting because it was too dangerous for Jews to be out. I didn't know where they were.

To make matters worse, I developed terrible asthma and would wake up in the middle of the night gasping for breath. Then more than ever I wanted my mother.

20

After a year in the orphanage I was removed for no reason I understood and sent to live with my godparents, who had a son my age. One weekend the family had to go somewhere, and I stayed with their maid. Before they left, they specifically said to me, "Don't leave the house."

The maid didn't know I was Jewish and saw that I was bored. She told me to go bike riding in the park, and I did. While I was riding around with another boy I met there, I suddenly spotted the Gestapo at the park gates. In terror I said to the boy, "Race you out!" and ducked my head low as I zoomed past the Germans. I escaped in time, but I was in a panic. I couldn't remember how to get back to my godparents' house. What should have taken a few minutes instead took two hours.

With the Germans close by, it wasn't safe for me to stay with my godparents anymore. So arrangements were made for me to go to a Protestant religious school. This school was run like a military academy, and I was forced to learn, whether I wanted to or not.

By then my asthma was much worse and I was sent to a doctor. He told me to drop my pants so he could give me an injection. When he saw that I was circumcised, he asked, "Are you Jewish?"

"No," I said with a straight face.

A week later, while I was in bed in the midst of another asthma attack, one of the brothers who taught us rushed into my room and hurriedly dressed me. "The Gestapo is searching the school," he said. He put me on a bike, handed me an address, and said, "Go quickly!"

I was ten years old then and small for my age. The bicycle seat was so high, I had to pedal standing, through two villages. When I finally found the right house, I knocked on the door, gasping for breath.

The couple inside received me royally. They made me such a delicious dinner, I forgot about my fear and my asthma got better.

The following day the man who was hiding my mother came and took me to his villa. For the next three weeks I was with my mother and was happy. But this man said it wasn't safe for him to be hiding a child, and I had to go to another religious school, this time in France. Until arrangements were made to get me there, I would be living with a business acquaintance of his and his wife.

This couple's names were Ademar and Louise Phillipp. They didn't know I was Jewish. I overheard the man tell them that my father was in the underground and was being hunted by the Germans. In truth, I didn't know where my father was. And now I didn't know when I'd see my mother again.

Ademar and Louise said that three years before, their only son had died from an illness at age fourteen. They were thrilled to have another boy in the house. They fed me so much food, I thought I was in heaven. When the time came for me to go to the school, I didn't want to leave.

"Pierrot [a fond way of saying Pierre], you can stay with us if you want," Ademar said to me. I flew into his arms and hugged him tightly.

The Phillipps said that in front of people I should refer to them as my aunt and uncle, but in the house I could use whatever names I chose. I made up "Titine" for Louise, and Ademar became "Peper," a word like "grandpa" because he reminded me of my own grandfather.

From the start they treated me like a king. They bought me clothes and shoes and let me decide what we should eat for dinner. Right away I felt at home with them.

Peper worked very hard as a farmer. When I asked him to teach me how to milk a cow or how to attach the carriage to the horse, he patiently showed me what to do. He never gave me chores. I helped only when I wanted to.

Titine didn't ask anything from me either. Yet whenever I woke up with an asthma attack, she'd sit with me through the night until she couldn't keep her eyes open. I felt as though I was their adopted child.

Meanwhile I wasn't sure if they or their relatives we visited once a week realized I was Jewish. Everybody was always nice to me, and no one ever said a bad word about Jews when I was around. Still, I wasn't about to take chances, and always bathed and got dressed in private.

Once it was settled that I was staying with them, Peper and Titine put me in school. By then I had missed so much, I had a difficult time keeping up. Also, my mind was somewhere else. I kept thinking about those times I had almost been caught by the Gestapo and wondering if it would happen again. I worried about my parents too. From time to time my mother sent me letters, so I knew she was alive. But there was no news about my father.

Then, one night in the summer of 1944, we were awakened by the sounds of trucks and loud knocking on the door. It was the fighting SS, who had picked our house, the largest in the area, to set up their headquarters. Up until now there had been no Germans in our village.

When the Germans saw there were two beds in my room, a soldier immediately claimed one. He was an important officer, and he was going to sleep next to me with a guard posted in front of the door. I was terrified.

In French this officer asked my name and my relationship to these people I was living with. I said they were my aunt and uncle, but I sensed he didn't believe me, since I looked Jewish with my dark hair and dark eyes. Titine and Peper were scared too, especially after I sneaked into the Germans' truck and stole some candies.

A week later more German soldiers came, many of whom were older than those in the first group. They were happy to see a kid, and joked with me. When nobody was around, they begged Titine for warm milk and bread.

The soldiers told Titine they couldn't wait until the war was over, and said they felt that Hitler was finished. We believed them because in the distance we could see defeated Germans in trucks and tanks coming back from France.

Then, one afternoon while I was outside, Americans began bombing the area. In horror, I tried to race to the house in between machine-gun holes that surrounded me. Miraculously I made it home in one piece.

When the bombing stopped and the German soldiers saw that I was alive, they kept rubbing me for good luck. They were ecstatic that I wasn't hurt and gave me chocolate. That night Titine made soup for everyone to celebrate my being alive.

Finally, in early September 1944, the Americans liberated our village. The Germans left, and the Americans came to stay with us. One soldier told me in Yiddish and then in German that he was Jewish and asked if I was too. I said, "Yes, I am a Jew," and looked at Titine and Peper when I said it. Now that it was out in the open, I wondered how they felt about me.

The soldier called over his friends to introduce them to the first Jewish child they had seen since the war began. Everyone was excited. Peper served champagne and we had a party.

The following day my mother bicycled over to the farm. She told me that for the past few months she had been staying in the village next to mine, but it had been too dangerous to get in touch with me.

When I saw her, I was happy and at the same time confused. I loved Titine and Peper and didn't want to leave them. Yet I wasn't ready to lose my mother.

Titine and Peper didn't want to lose me either. They asked my mother if they could adopt me, but she said no. She did say I could stay with the Phillipps a little longer while she got settled in Brussels. So l lived on the farm for another few months until my mother got a job and found us a small apartment. All this time there was no word about my father. We learned later that he had died in a concentration camp.

Finally my mother came for me, and I had to say goodbye to Titine and Peper. It was hard for the three of us to part. I didn't want to separate from them, their house, and the comforts they gave me. We had become a family.

Over the years I kept calling and writing to them, and on every holiday I automatically went to the farm for my vacation. I loved them so much.

Once when we were together, I asked when they had realized I was Jewish. They said they had sensed it early on but didn't think much about it. Later, when they found out for sure that I was Jewish, they still wanted to adopt me. On the one hand, I wished they could have been my parents. My life would have been easier with two parents and away from the problems of the city. On the other hand, I wanted to be with my mother.

In 1948 my mother remarried, and three years later we went to America. This time leaving Titine and Peper was even more difficult. We knew that living so far apart, we could never be as close as before. When I hugged them good-bye, I felt sick inside. They were such special people.

*Kurt in 1993.*

POSTSCRIPT

Even though I continued to write and telephone Titine and Peper, it wasn't the same anymore. I knew that when I left Belgium, their hearts were broken. Not long after, they both got sick and died, one right after the other. I felt as if I had lost my other set of parents.

I still think about Titine and Peper, and today more than ever I realize how much I loved them. What they did for me was remarkable. They were like saints. I could never thank them enough.

*Kurt sells antique jewelry.*

27

*Rose Silberberg-Skier, age 12, at displaced persons' camp in 1946.*

# Rose Silberberg-Skier

POLAND

## "We always had to be silent"

I come from an enormous family of Hasidic Jews who were very, very religious. Generations back, one of my relatives was a famous rabbi. Until the Germans invaded Poland, we all lived near my grandfather, an hour away from the city of Krakow. Every Saturday after synagogue the grandchildren would gather at his house and line up for a chocolate wrapped in fancy paper.

Both my father and my mother worked in my grandfather's printing business. While they were away, a maid took care of me. On Sundays, without anyone knowing, she took me to church with her. I'd chant the prayers and stare at the beautiful statues.

In 1939, when I was five and my sister Mala was an infant, the Germans invaded Poland. Word soon spread that they were shooting the Jewish men in the small towns and villages. My father said we should go to the city, where he thought it would be safer. When we returned to our town, we found that many of my uncles had been killed.

Meanwhile my grandfather, a widower, had left for Palestine hoping to get homes for us there. By the time arrangements were made, the British, who governed Palestine,

29

wouldn't let more Jews in. So my grandfather stayed there while we were stuck in Poland.

First the Germans forced us and thousands of other Jews into the Srodula Ghetto in one of the poorest Polish neighborhoods. They gave the Poles our beautiful homes and shoved us into tiny shacks. We were seventeen people in two rooms. The only way we could get food was by bribing the Germans with jewelry and other valuable possessions. Others, who weren't lucky enough to have anything to trade, died of starvation.

In the ghetto the Germans kept announcing that parents should send their children to the Jewish-run school, but my parents decided to teach me reading and arithmetic at home. One day the Germans surrounded the school and took all the children away.

When my father realized how dangerous things were, he contacted a Polish woman he knew named Stanislawa Cicha and offered to pay her for hiding us in the chicken coop connected to her house. Mrs. Cicha agreed, and my father quickly began to make the coop livable.

At this time you could still leave the ghetto before curfew, so my father worked on the coop in every spare moment. First he boarded up its only window so no one would see what he was doing. Then he furnished it with a small table, some chairs, and pads for us to sleep on. He also built a tiny bunker under the floor for added safety and piled potatoes on top of the trap door to mask it. The bunker was windowless, with only enough air to breathe for a few hours, but in an emergency it would protect us.

Finally everything was ready, and the four of us and my Uncle Israel slipped out of the ghetto in the middle of the night. We began living in the cramped coop, which was dark and smelled from the chickens that Mrs. Cicha used to keep.

From the beginning we depended totally on Mrs. Cicha. She brought us our food and water and emptied the pail we used as a toilet. If the time ever came for us to hide in the bunker, she'd be the one who'd lift open the trap door to let us out.

Mrs. Cicha was originally from Lithuania and was married to a Polish man who was now in a labor camp in Germany. She had no children, no close friends, and no relatives living nearby. Except for her dog, Rex, and the rabbits, turtles, and cats she kept inside with her, she was alone.

But she had a neighbor in the house attached to hers. This woman, Mrs. Dudwalka, hated Jews. If she had known we were in the coop, she gladly would have turned us in. All day she sat at her window watching people go by, so we never went out.

And we always had to be silent. Even walking on the wooden floor was dangerous, because the planks creaked and that noise might arouse Mrs. Dudwalka's suspicion. Besides, Mrs. Cicha was a seamstress, and her customers came to the house to have their clothes fixed. When they were around, we went barefoot or sat in one place for hours.

My sister by then was only two and a half and didn't understand why she couldn't run about or speak above a whisper. No matter how hard my parents tried to discourage her, Mala kept climbing up to the coop's tiny hayloft and singing in a loud voice. Finally, to protect all of us, my father asked a Polish family he knew if they could hide her.

31

He told them that my Aunt Sara Wachsman, who was passing as a Christian, would bring them money each month.

This couple had two teenage sons and were delighted to have a little girl in the house, but they had to be careful. They said they were willing to take Mala if they could change her name to Mary and after the war convert her to Catholicism. They also wanted my father to promise that one day Mala could marry one of their sons. My Orthodox father had a difficult time making a decision. In the end, he agreed.

By then food was scarce. Mrs. Cicha's coupons barely got enough for her, and with us to feed it was even harder. Sometimes she bought things on the black market, but that wasn't safe because people might notice her carrying home too much.

It hurt my father to see us go hungry. And he hated living in the coop. When Aunt Sara told him that the Germans were giving out food coupons to ghetto Jews who registered for identification papers, he said we should go back there.

My mother thought it was a bad idea but gave in. Finally the two of them and Uncle Israel left for a few days to see how things were. While they were gone, Aunt Sara stayed with me.

The ghetto had quieted down, so my parents stayed there. Usually Aunt Sara kept me company, but sometimes she too disappeared, and then I was alone in the coop. I was terrified. Every strange noise made me think someone was coming to get me.

At night, Mrs. Cicha brought me food, and I'd whisper to her how horrible I felt. She'd say, "Don't worry. Things will get better." But I didn't believe her.

*Stanislawa Cicha.*

To keep me busy, Mrs. Cicha gave me a pen and paper, and I wrote letters and drew pictures, which Aunt Sara delivered to my parents. I also read and reread the books my parents had left for me. A while back my mother had found an empty German cigarette carton that had swastikas on one side and was plain on the other. I cut the carton into a lot of pieces and made playing cards with them, drawing a chicken for the queen and a rooster for the king. But I was bored and lonely. I missed my mother.

Once my parents came to the coop for a short stay. I heard

33

my mother press my father not to go back to the ghetto. She said it was getting more and more dangerous there and, also, she didn't like leaving me by myself. But my father wouldn't listen. Instead he suggested I come now and then to stay with them.

So at night, in the spring and summer of 1943, Aunt Sara would sneak me into the ghetto, and I'd spend a week or two with my parents. After being shut up in the tiny dark coop, the ghetto was a treat. There were other nine-year-olds to play with, and I could go outdoors.

One Sabbath in July when I wasn't scheduled to visit my parents, I begged Aunt Sara to take me anyhow so I could spend Shabbat with them, and she did. The next morning when I awoke, the ghetto was surrounded by the SS with guns pointed in every window. On loudspeakers they said that all Jews were being sent to work camps and should go to the train station.

My father knew about a bunker that was entered through a stove, and we crawled in, one after another, with thirteen people following behind. But the SS dogs soon found us, and we had to come out.

By then the trains to the camps were filled, so we were told to wait in our room until the next day. Since Aunt Sara had Christian papers and fair hair and I was blue-eyed, my father thought we could pass as Gentiles and might be able to escape. But with his heavy Yiddish accent and he and my mother not having Aryan papers, he felt they had no chance.

He told us about another bunker, which was above a chandelier and was stocked with food. We could hide there for a few days until things were safe. Then he made me recite the address of cousins in Jerusalem and said that after the war, I should find a way to get to them. "I will try to come too, but if not, they will take care of you. Your job is to remember you are Jewish."

The next morning my mother hugged me good-bye and promised me we'd see each other again. As she and my father walked in one direction, Aunt Sara and I went in the other. I looked back to see my mother's face once more, but only my father turned around for a moment.

There were sixteeen of us crammed into the attic above the chandelier. It was very hot, and we had no water. Through a hole in the wall we could see the SS running around below, emptying the ghetto of thousands of Jews.

Suddenly one man in the bunker, who had watched his baby killed by the Nazis, decided to give himself up. No one could change his mind. When he lowered the chandelier to climb out, the SS saw him. In seconds they directed their machine guns at us. I was so petrified, I couldn't move or speak. I thought this was the end.

We were all taken to a hospital to wait there for a van that would take us to Auschwitz concentration camp, ten miles away. "Do you want to live?" Aunt Sara asked me. I shook my head yes. "Then you've got to escape," she said. She brought me to a window and pointed out the road to Mrs. Cicha's house.

But I had never traveled alone in the city, and I didn't know what Mrs. Cicha's house looked like in the daylight. I was scared.

Aunt Sara spoke to Mr. Feder, a Jewish man she knew in the hospital who was being forced by the Germans to work as a policeman. She offered him a diamond to let me out, but first he made her give him Mrs. Cicha's address so he and his wife could escape there too.

For the next five hours I crawled on my hands and knees through tall grass along a ravine, trying to keep out of sight of the SS. When I was about to cross the bridge leading to the Christian sector, some Polish teenagers who should not have been on the Jewish side started tormenting me with their dog. "It's a Jew! It's a Jew!" they shouted. "Let's call the SS." I thought, *Now* my life is over.

Suddenly out of nowhere a Polish woman appeared and yelled at the boys to leave me alone. She told me where to find the nearest streetcar and said I should get moving quickly. It was Sunday, and Aunt Sara had reminded me that Catholic children would be coming from church wearing clean clothes. She said I should pick some wildflowers and use them to hide my dirty face and dress. Hurriedly I did this.

When I finally got to Mrs. Cicha's door, I was trembling. She pulled me in and asked where the others were. Then she gave me water to wash myself and took me into the coop. My Uncle Sam Klapholz and Uncle Israel, who both had escaped from the ghetto, were there, but not my parents. I was afraid to think where they could be.

A few days later Mr. Feder came with his wife, and then Aunt Sara arrived with Aunt Bela. Right after that other Jews who knew Mrs. Cicha came too. There were sixteen of us in that little space.

Mrs. Cicha couldn't possibly feed us all. Once a week she brought some food that Aunt Sara cooked on a small stove, but the rest of the time we had only bread. The limit for each person was two slices a day. I cut mine into a hundred tiny pieces and every ten minutes ate a morsel to make it last longer.

Meanwhile my parents still had not come. I kept looking at a picture of my mother that I had with me and couldn't stop whimpering.

Then unexpectedly, in January 1944, the family who had been hiding Mala brought her to the house. They said they couldn't keep my sister anymore because their neighbors suspected she was Jewish and had threatened to call the Gestapo. Mala was now four and a half. As soon as she saw me, she rushed into my arms and whispered in my ear, "I can tell *you* that I'm Jewish."

This time I was determined not to let anyone take Mala away again. The minute she sneezed or coughed, I rushed to cover her mouth, petrified someone would hear her. If she climbed up to the tiny hayloft, I quickly grabbed her and told her to sit still.

Five weeks after Mala arrived, Aunt Bela got a letter from her husband, who was in a concentration camp. It was delivered by a Polish foreman who worked there and said that my uncle was alive. Aunt Bela wrote a note back in Yiddish and gave it to the foreman.

A few days later, in the middle of the night, there was loud banging on Mrs. Cicha's door. From the coop I heard SS men shouting, "Where's the Jewish woman?" They had stopped the Polish foreman to check his identification and found Aunt Bela's letter on him.

Within seconds Uncle Israel pushed open the boarded window of the coop and jumped out, while Uncle Sam threw me into the bunker. After he helped Aunt Sara and Aunt

Bela down, he closed the trap door, piled up the potatoes, and left through the window. Suddenly from above I heard Mala crying, "I want my sister." In the confusion my Uncle Israel, who was responsible for hiding Mala, had panicked and forgotten her.

The SS men came into the coop and grabbed Mala. It was winter, and Mala wasn't even wearing a coat or shoes. They also arrested seven of the others, who weren't able to get out in time. They took Mrs. Cicha, too. Then they boarded up the house.

For an hour Aunt Sara, Aunt Bela, and I waited in the bunker, wondering who'd come to lift open the trap door for us. We were so worried. Finally Uncle Sam let us out. He had taken a huge chance coming back to the house but said he could never forgive himself if he left us there.

He advised Aunt Sara and me to go to a Polish woman he knew to get false passports and new identity papers. The man who forged the papers wrote that we were Christian and that I was Aunt Sara's daughter. He suggested we go to Germany where they were hiring Polish women to work and Aunt Sara could pass as one of them.

In Germany Aunt Sara was assigned a job in a convent and I, as her daughter, was allowed to stay with her. But because I wasn't German, I couldn't go to school or eat with the children. Instead I cut beans and served the meals.

Three days after we arrived, the SS came to the convent to arrest us. As we were being dragged out, the nuns wondered what was going on. And we wondered who could have turned us in.

For six hours the Gestapo questioned us at their headquarters, accusing us of being Jewish. But Aunt Sara and I insisted we weren't. Then an SS man took me into the corridor and pointed a revolver at my head. "If you tell me you're Jewish, I'll let you go," he said. But I refused to be tricked.

Finally he made me recite Catholic prayers to prove I was Christian. I remembered them from when my Polish maid had taken me to church with her, and rattled them off. I so convinced the SS man, he let Aunt Sara and me go free. But every day the SS called the convent to see if we were still there.

In January 1945 the Americans and British started bombing the area. Although I was happy the Allies had come, I thought now we'd really be killed. Then one day in April it was quiet outside. Cautiously everyone crawled out of the shelter. The Germans were gone and the road was filled with Russian soldiers. I felt as though the Messiah had come. For the first time since the war had begun, I knew I was going to live.

That day Aunt Sara and I started back to Poland, where the war had ended a few months before. When we got there, we went to my grandfather's house, hoping my parents and sister would be waiting. Instead, Polish people were living in the house. They said we should leave the town quickly because anti-Semitic Poles were killing Jews in large numbers.

We had no money and nowhere to stay. Aunt Sara decided to put me in an orphanage until she got settled. I had never been sick all the time I had been in the coop, but in the orphanage I caught measles and then whooping cough.

Meanwhile I kept reading the lists posted in the yard to see if my parents' and sister's names were among those who had survived the concentration camps. But none of them was ever mentioned.

That November Aunt Sara came for me, and together we went to a displacement camp in the American sector of Germany. Before we left Poland, we said good-bye to Mrs. Cicha. She told us she had been sent to Auschwitz and the family who had hidden Mala had been denounced by their neighbors and sent there too. They all had survived, but not Mala, who was shot by the Germans almost as soon as she arrived in the camp. Later I learned from a cousin who had been with my parents that they too had died.

Now there was no reason for Aunt Sara and me to stay in Europe, so we applied to go to the United States. It took six years for us to get our papers. During that time I lived in the displaced persons' camp and went to school. I never saw Mrs. Cicha again.


POSTSCRIPT

When I came to the United States, I wrote to Mrs. Cicha, and over the years I sent her letters and photos of myself with my husband and three children. She always wrote back and sent pictures of herself and the house where I had been hidden.

I never asked her why she had taken such an enormous risk hiding me and all the others. I know it wasn't for the money. And it wasn't because she particularly liked Jews. She could have taken them or left them.

*Rose in 1993.*

I think she was the kind of person who did what she believed and wasn't influenced by others. She had guts. If it wasn't for her, a rare individual, and God watching over me, I wouldn't be here today.

*Mrs. Cicha has been honored at Yad Vashem, and when she was alive, the State of Israel sent her money to make her life easier. She died a few years ago.*

*Rose owns a video store and works there.*

41

*Manny Stern, age 7 (left), with brother, Sammy,
and sister, Esther.*

# MANNY STERN

## *"I hated being by myself"*

I was the oldest of three kids and grew up in an Orthodox family in Antwerp, Belgium. Every Shabbat I went to synagogue with my father, and during the week I went to a religious school.

In May 1940, when I was seven, the Germans invaded Belgium. Whenever I heard the air raid sirens, I ran into the street to watch the bombs fall from the sky.

Soon the bombing became unbearable, and my parents said we were going to southern France where it was safer. My mother carefully packed our Sabbath candlesticks, and my father laid his Tallit in the suitcase.

While we were traveling, German planes strafed our train. Every few minutes the train stopped, and all the passengers frantically scrambled under the cars for protection. When I saw how scared the grown-ups were, I got frightened too.

Finally we settled in a little town called Bousquet-d'Orb where lots of our relatives were staying. We lived there for the next two years, and I went to school. I was not afraid to be a Jew.

But by the end of 1942 the French police started rounding up Jews for the Germans to send to labor camps, and my father was taken away. My mother, my younger sister, Esther, my Uncle Maurice who was sixteen, and I were forced to go to a transit camp where Jews were being shipped out every day. My four-year-old brother, Sammy, was safe in a summer camp connected to a convent.

From the look on my mother's face, I knew we were in trouble. One day she told Esther and me that a woman from the Red Cross was going to help the two of us escape. Then she kissed us good-bye.

We followed the woman under barbed wire and through fields until she brought us back to Bousquet-d'Orb, where I was amazed to see my parents and Sammy again. My father told us he had jumped off the train that was headed for Germany. And my mother had left the camp when her brother, Uncle Maurice, convinced a French doctor that she was pregnant and should be released. They shipped Uncle Maurice out in her place.

Now we all had to hide from the Germans. My parents said it would be safer if we were hidden separately and consulted my seventeen-year-old Aunt Frida, who was passing as a Christian. She got in touch with the local priest, who made arrangements for Esther and me to live with different farm families. Sammy was going to a convent.

The priest took us to our new homes. My family's last name was Fabaron, and I became Hubert Fabaron, their nephew from another part of France. The Fabarons lived in an isolated part of France where there were no Jews, but both Aunt Frida and the priest warned me to be careful nevertheless. You never knew who might turn you in, they said.

The Fabarons also kept reminding me to keep my Judaism a secret. They told me again and again that if they were found hiding a Jew they would be shot.

Meanwhile I was enrolled in the local school, and every day I walked the four miles there and back by myself. Since our farm was the only one in the area, I never saw another child except in class. After I had been in school one month, the Fabarons pulled me out. They had heard that some of the teachers were collaborating with the Germans and were afraid I might be denounced.

From then on Madame Fabaron gave me informal lessons at home, and on Sundays she taught me the catechism. Although she and her husband were Protestant and not at all religious, they felt I should learn about Christianity in case I was ever questioned.

The Fabarons told me they were originally from the city, where he had been an engineer and she a teacher. One day they gave it all up and bought a farm. Now they were in their sixties and had a married son who helped them with the chores.

Except for those three adults, I rarely saw another human being. Esther was twenty miles away, and with dirt roads between us, it was difficult to see each other. Luckily the Fabarons had a big library, and I spent my time devouring their books.

One day, though, Esther arrived in a wagon with the woman who was hiding her. The woman wanted me to talk to my sister because she wasn't eating. Esther confided that most of the food served on the farm was pork, and in our Orthodox Jewish home that wasn't allowed. Although my seven-year-old sister was hungry, she was afraid to go against our religion.

I knew that with the food shortages we couldn't be choosey, and I told this to Esther. After that she ate whatever they gave her.

In springtime my job on the farm was tending the sheep and goats. At four or five in the morning I woke up, had a cup of black coffee, and took the animals to the field. For hours I sat under a tree, reading one book after another.

Around eight in the morning Madame Fabaron arrived with a big bowl of café au lait (coffee with milk) and some bread. Then at lunchtime she brought me homemade sausage and more bread. I never went hungry. But I hated being by myself. Even in the house, I didn't have much to say to the elderly couple. To make it worse, there was no electricity or telephone.

Besides tending the flocks, I also took care of the vineyards. In the summer I marched barefoot in tubs filled with grapes to press them. In the winter Monsieur Fabaron taught me how to set traps for rabbits, collect the animals, and skin them.

Nothing on the farm was done by machinery, and everything took a lot of time. It was a rigorous life, but working alongside Madame or Monsieur Fabaron made me feel I was part of the family. Even though Monsieur Fabaron was gruff and neither of the two was affectionate, they were nice to me and made me feel safe. But I was always lonely, except every now and then when a stream of young men came to stay with us.

They were the French Maquis, the underground, who were working against the Germans. Our farm was their headquarters in southern France. The Maquis carried guns and looked very important. Whenever they were around, life seemed exciting.

Once they brought with them a Jewish man who was an expert forger. All day long he hid in a room, writing and signing false papers that the Maquis later distributed to Jews who were trying to escape or pass as Gentiles.

The Maquis always treated me like one of them. They made me their lookout and sat me high in a tree on the top of a hill where I could see fifteen to twenty miles in the distance. If I spotted the French police on the road, I was to alert them immediately.

When the Maquis were nearby, I was never afraid and acted as cocky as they did. I wished they could stay forever, but after a few days they always moved on.

When I was ten and had been with the Fabarons for about a year, Aunt Frida arrived and asked if I wanted to go to Switzerland with my parents. She told me that my mother had a baby named Susie and that they and my father were hiding in France, in the foothills of the Alps. Now they were collecting my brother Sammy and were going to try to escape. From what I understood, crossing into Switzerland was dangerous, and I didn't want to be put in that kind of situation again. So I decided to stay with the Fabarons. Esther too didn't want to leave her family.

At least now I knew my parents were alive. Until then I was too afraid to think about them and just concentrated on myself. I was sad that I wasn't having fun with kids my age. While the Fabarons were kind to me, their life was strict and severe. They didn't even celebrate holidays or birthdays.

To make matters worse, they didn't like Jews. In front of me, they made negative comments about them. But they also talked about how they hated the Germans. They were angry that the Germans had invaded their country and were dictating what people should do. Nobody was going to push the Fabarons around. They strongly cherished their independence. I think that's why they took me in.

When I had been with the Fabarons for a year and a half, the Maquis started talking about an expected Allied landing in southern France. Now the Maquis' mission was to disrupt transportation so the Germans couldn't reinforce their troops. They described how they were blowing up trains and bridges and raiding depots. To me it sounded like an exciting adventure story. I was not the least bit afraid.

Then suddenly, in the summer of 1944, the Germans began pouring a lot of reinforcements into our area. One day when I was posted as the lookout, I saw many, many German vehicles coming up the road. Quickly I ran to tell this to the Maquis, and within seconds everyone cleared out of the farmhouse. The Fabarons said I should hide in the fields, and they and the Maquis scattered in different directions.

For hours I lay perfectly still with my ear to the ground, listening to the rumble of German tanks in the distance. I was petrified as I waited for the German convoy to pass. I hoped they wouldn't destroy our farmhouse. And I prayed these Germans wouldn't take Jews.

Eventually all was quiet and we were safe, but I was shaken from the experience. It made me think back to the terror I felt when I had hidden with my family under the train as we escaped from Belgium.

Right after that, France was liberated. I didn't even know what the date was. After being so isolated and concentrating all my energy on day-to-day survival, I had lost all sense of time. But now I was free, and I finally let myself think about my parents. I wondered if they had made it safely to Switzerland and felt scared thinking that they might not have.

Some weeks later a young rabbi came to the farm. He said he was gathering Jewish children who had been hidden and was taking them to a large house where he would train them to become Jews again. He said he was going to get Esther next.

When I heard that I had to leave the Fabarons, I was devastated. I had become very dependent on them and felt secure in their home. I didn't want to say good-bye. And they had trouble parting from me.

At least in Rabbi Soil's house I was reunited with my sister. For the next nine months we lived with thirty to forty other children in a scout-camp setting. With Rabbi Soil as leader we hiked arm in arm into the mountains, where he taught us how to pray and to read Hebrew again. It was amazing how much I had forgotten.

I loved how Rabbi Soil made learning fun. Yet I always had my parents in the back of my mind. I wondered how they would ever find me. Little by little, other families came to get their children, but mine didn't show up. I was very concerned.

Then one day I got word from Aunt Frida that my mother

and father were alive and would be coming for me soon. And eventually my father did arrive. He said that he and my mother had to wait in Switzerland until the war was over throughout Europe.

He took Esther and me by train to Antwerp to join the rest of my family. Except for Uncle Maurice, we had all survived the war. I should have been overjoyed to see everyone, but instead I stood there numb. I was too drained from the whole war experience.

My family stayed in Antwerp for the next year and a half, but life was tough there. Finally we moved to the United States. With all these changes, I didn't think about the Fabarons again until I was in my late teens. By then I realized they would be in their eighties and thought they must be dead. So I didn't contact them.

Still, I never forgot what they had done for me. The older I became, the more I understood that if they hadn't taken me in, I wouldn't be alive. Deep down I felt I owed my life to them. They were unusual people.

*Manny Stern in 1993.*

POSTSCRIPT

Today the Fabarons would be over one hundred years old. Even when I lived with them, they weren't young. Yet they were willing to take on the burden of a young Jewish child and endanger their own lives.

In my mind they were the real heroes of the war. Too bad there weren't more people like them.

*Until twenty years ago, Manny was a physicist. Now he's involved in businesses connected with food.*

51

*Charly, Cécile, and Anny Rojer in 1940,*
*before going into hiding.*

# CÉCILE ROJER JERUCHIM

BELGIUM

*"With my sister nearby,
I felt less lonely"*

I grew up outside of Brussels, Belgium, in a town where we were the only Jewish family. We were not at all religious. On Saturday we went to the opera instead of synagogue. Yet whenever there were fights between kids on our street, I was called "dirty Jew."

Still, I thought of myself first as a Belgian. In school I sang anti-German songs along with everyone else because we had learned that throughout history the Germans had invaded our country. In 1940, when they again occupied Belgium, I thought I'd be treated like any other Belgian child. But two years later, when I was eleven, I was singled out because I was a Jew. I had to wear a star on my clothing and I couldn't go to school anymore or take dancing lessons.

By October it had become so dangerous for Jews that my parents paid a tuberculosis sanitarium to hide my six-year-old brother, Charly. Next they tried to find a safe place for me and my sister, Anny, who was thirteen and a half. In January, before final plans were made for us, my parents were arrested.

For the following three days Anny and I stayed at the house of my Gentile friend, whose parents didn't know what to do with us. Finally they said that the nursing home down

53

the street was willing to hide us. During curfew, in the pitch dark, Anny and I walked there by ourselves. We knew if we were caught we'd be shot.

As soon as we got there, the nurses quickly showed us to a room that had a huge sign on the door saying CONTAGIOUS. They told us to get into bed and to pretend we were very sick.

Both Anny and I loved acting, but this time we were scared. Whenever the Germans came to search, we lay frozen, a thermometer propped in each of our mouths by a nurse so we couldn't talk. Luckily the Germans were afraid they'd catch our disease and left us alone.

After we had been in the nursing home for two months, we were told that we were going to a safer place. A woman we had never met before took us by train to a mansion on the border of France and Belgium. It was owned by a baron and baroness, who had converted the stable into dormitories to house city children during month-long retreats from war-torn areas.

Anny and I, however, stayed from March to August. If kids asked why we weren't going home, we said our parents had been killed in the war and we were orphans.

In the dormitory there was a counselor named Renée whom I particularly liked. I wasn't sure if she realized I was Jewish, but still she was kind to me. When I told her I was worried about Charly (I was sure my parents couldn't afford to pay the sanitarium anymore), she said she'd help me find him.

Meanwhile, three mornings a week, at the crack of dawn, we had to go to church. Anny and I didn't have warm clothing and sat freezing in the unheated stone building.

It made us miserable. We also hated getting up so early.

In the middle of one night I suddenly had an idea. I woke my sister, winked at her, then started "sleepwalking" through the dormitory. In a frenzy I jumped from bed to bed. The girls and the counselors got scared, thinking something was very wrong with me. No one dared to wake me.

When morning came, the counselors said I should stay back from church to catch up on my sleep, and they told Anny to keep me company in case I walked in my sleep again.

A few nights later I "sleepwalked" into the kitchen and helped myself and the other kids to food. Again no one stopped me. But when this went on for a few more nights, I was sent to a vet, the only doctor in town. He examined me and asked Anny if mental illness ran in our family. Anny said she thought so. The doctor gave me enormous pills, probably meant for a horse, which he said would calm me down. Of course I didn't take them.

Other than these night episodes, my life at the mansion was boring. I didn't go to school, and there were no books to read. I had plenty of time to think about my parents. I felt they must be prisoners in Germany, and when the war was over I'd see them again. I missed them, but with my sister nearby I felt less lonely.

In August, without being given a reason, Anny and I were sent from the mansion to the Convent of Pity, in the Flemish part of Belgium. This was a poor convent that took in orphans and children of unwed mothers. I was now twelve and attended the school there. But Anny, at fourteen, was too old and instead had to work in the laundry, scrubbing clothes by hand.

*Cécile (top row, third from left) at the Convent of Pity.*

In my classes at the convent I mostly learned about the saints. And at mass every morning and in church on Sunday I was surrounded by the saints too. My life was filled with religion. Like the other girls, I knelt when I prayed, but because I hadn't been baptized, I wasn't allowed to take Communion. When the girls asked me why, I said my parents had died when I was very young.

Meanwhile Anny and I noticed that there were about ten other girls who also weren't waiting in line for the wafer. We figured out that they must be Jewish too. Without ever discussing our family backgrounds, we soon formed our own group.

Every few months the girls in the convent had visitors. On that day a nun would call someone's name and say, "Your aunt is waiting for you in the auditorium." Of course, nobody ever came to see the Jewish children, but there were plenty of orphan boarders so we didn't seem odd. Still, when the visitors left and the girls returned with candy, we were jealous.

One nun, Clotilde, knew which children were Jewish. She even asked me to teach her Yiddish words. After visiting day, when the lights were dimmed, she walked down the dormitory aisle to say good night to each of us. When she came to my bed, she leaned over and put a candy in my mouth. In Yiddish she said, "Sleep well, my child."

Clotilde was affectionate and gave me more attention than the other nuns did. But with so many girls to look after, she couldn't give that much. Although I told her a little bit about my mother and how she made a big fuss over birthdays, Clotilde didn't know a lot about my family or how I was feeling.

Especially at night, I was sad remembering how my parents had been ripped away from me. Sometimes I cried myself to sleep, and I started wetting my bed.

Praying to the saints, though, gave me comfort. It was the only thing that calmed me. Soon I started to believe in them and the Virgin Mary.

One day when I heard a nun say that baptism classes were being given, I decided to take them. I wanted to be a Christian. Also I knew that on baptism day I'd get a nice meal that included a hard-boiled egg. I was always starving. And when I became a Catholic, I could join the Girl Scouts too. That meant that once a week I could get away from the convent with a lay leader and go on hikes with other girls.

I lived by the rules. I had to dress a certain way, get up and go to bed at a certain time, and be quiet. From minute to minute I knew exactly what I'd be doing, and that the nuns as my guardians would be overseeing things. When I was with my parents, my life was not at all rigid, and I would have hated this kind of routine. But after being shifted from one place to another, I felt secure with the same people and looked forward to three meals a day even if it was only a little turnip on my plate.

That doesn't mean I didn't have fun. In the dormitory, when the nuns weren't around, Anny and I would put on skits. We became known as the entertainment sisters. When we mopped the hallways we horsed around too, unless we saw a nun coming.

But each day the war continued, my life became harder. There was barely any food, and I was always cold. In winter I had no gloves and developed an infectious rash on my hands. Other kids got boils.

The worst part was the Allied bombing that started in Belgium in the spring of 1944. It was very scary. At the same time, Germans who were now stationed close by began to make inspections of the convent. All of us were terrified, remembering what we had learned about Germany in our classes.

The Germans were hungry, and sometimes they came to the convent for a meal. When they'd stop me in the hall to say hello in French, I'd answer back politely, but I was always petrified.

During this time I didn't know what was happening to the Jews. Neither did anyone else in the convent, having no radio or newspapers. We thought they were prisoners and were being treated like every other Belgian in captivity.

Finally, in September 1944, Belgium was liberated. I was

so happy when I saw American soldiers comimg down the street, I shouted *"Vive Amérique"* and screamed for chewing gum. That night I told Clotilde my parents would probably be picking me up on October 4, my birthday.

October 4 came and went, and my parents didn't arrive. I was disappointed. Meanwhile some of the other Jewish children had left with their parents. I kept wondering, When will mine come for me? While I waited, I went on with my usual life.

Then one afternoon a nun told Anny and me that we had a visitor, Uncle Bernard, my mother's brother. Since he and my mother hadn't been close, I hardly knew him, but he strongly resembled her and I got a funny feeling inside when I saw him. Uncle Bernard said that as soon as he got settled with his own family, he would take Anny and me out of the convent. So Anny and I stayed at the convent for a few months longer.

After that we were temporarily placed with a Jewish family until an orphanage was opened for Jewish children whose parents had not come back from the war.

I went to live with the Greenbergs, who had known my parents, and Anny stayed nearby with another family we knew. This was the first time I had ever been separated from my sister. It was very difficult.

By now I was beginning to lose hope about my parents. Their names had never been mentioned on the lists of Jews who had survived the camps. More than ever before, I turned to Catholicism for comfort.

The first time the Greenbergs saw me cross myself, they were mortified. "You're a Jewish girl," they said, "and you have to behave like one." They immediately enrolled me in school where Yiddish was spoken, and within a few weeks I gave up Catholicism and became a Jew again.

All this time I had been wondering where my brother was. Then one day some kids knocked on the door, and there was a boy who looked familiar. "Are you Mademoiselle Cécile?" he asked in French.

"Charly!" I screamed.

He too was staying with a family nearby. When he told them his sisters' names, they had sent him to the Greenbergs' house because they thought he and I looked alike. That night the Greenbergs let Charly and Anny sleep over. We three stayed up for hours, laughing and crying. Charly said that after leaving the sanitarium, he went from one hiding place to another, and now he too was being sent to an orphanage, but not the same one Anny and I were going to.

In the meantime Uncle Bernard and his family had moved to the United States, and after we had been in the orphanage for two and a half years, he and other relatives got money together to send for us. I was sixteen and studying to be a teacher. I didn't want to leave Belgium and the friends I had made there.

I also worried that if my parents came back, they wouldn't be able to find me. But an aunt who was going to stay in Belgium said she would tell them where I was.

Before I sailed to the United States, I hitchhiked with a friend to the convent where Clotilde now was. She and I hugged and kissed, but we had little to talk about. That was the last time I ever saw or heard from her. Still, I always remembered how kind she was and how she and the other nuns kept me safe while the world was falling apart.

*Cécile in 1993.*

POSTSCRIPT

Twenty years ago, with my husband, Simon, I went back to Belgium and visited the area where I had lived with my parents. Since then, I've returned many times. The neighborhood looks the same, but whenever I'm there, I get sad.

I've also visited the Convent of Pity, which has a new name, and told a nun that I was a Jewish child hidden there during the war. She called in a young nun who said she had heard my story from the older nuns, and then she took me upstairs to see them. They were very feeble. When I asked about Clotilde, they said she had left the order.

I looked at these nuns and thought, They're responsible for my being alive. As a child, I didn't realize how much I owed to them. At one point I even thought they took me in because they got paid for it. But that wasn't at all how it was. They rescued me because they were good people who were willing to risk their lives for what they believed in.

*Cécile teaches aerobics.*

61

*Jacques van Dam, age 12$^{1}/_{2}$ in 1945.*

# Jacques van Dam

## *"I would have done anything to survive"*

I lived in a neighborhood in Amsterdam, Holland, where many of the people were Jewish. Although my family wasn't that religious, I took Hebrew lessons and sometimes went to shul with my father.

In May 1940, when I was almost eight, the Germans attacked Holland. My friends and I couldn't wait till the air raids were over so we could run into the street and collect the bombs' shells.

But two years later our telephone was taken away and then my bike. That's when I knew that we were in danger because we were Jews.

Meanwhile the Germans kept picking up Jewish children off the street, and Jews were being deported in full swing. That autumn my father sent me to northeastern Holland to live with the head of the company he had worked for. I was happy to get away from the tension of the city. But ten days later the man sent me back to my parents because he was afraid for his family's safety.

By then my father was working at night as an air raid warden in a hospital. It was an important job, so our whole family's identity papers were stamped *exempt from deporta-*

*tion until further notice.* Still, I was always nervous. Every day in school I'd see that more and more kids were missing and realize the Germans had taken them away.

Then suddenly, in February 1943, the Germans raided my father's hospital, rounding up all the wardens, even those with special identity papers. My father managed to escape and eventually get home, but he told us we all had to go into hiding.

Since he was active in the Dutch resistance, he knew a lot of non-Jews in the underground who could help us. They found a Dutch professor to hide my four-year-old sister, Helene, who didn't look Jewish, and she left on March 1. The next day I was to go to northern Holland, where the underground was planning to find a non-Jewish home for me. My parents said they'd be staying in a different part of Amsterdam with another Gentile family.

"To survive this war, you must do everything to keep your Judaism a secret," my parents explained to me, crying. They warned me that because I was circumcised I should never be seen nude. I was scared.

On March 2 a man I called "Uncle Willem" picked me up and took me to a couple whose last name was Koelewyn. The husband was the grounds- and gamekeeper for the royal family, and their house bordered on miles of woods. Every day when their eleven-year-old daughter, Annemarie, came home from school, we played there. The rest of the time I helped with the vegetable garden.

The Koelewyns were very nice, and I was happy with them until one afternoon at the end of the summer, when I heard shooting in the distance and shouts that the Germans were coming. Within seconds I slipped through the corn-fields and ran into the woods.

When I came to a small hut where food was left for the animals, I crawled inside and hid there. Every few minutes I peeked out to see if things had quieted down. Suddenly I heard a strange noise and thought it was someone coming to get me. In an instant I leaped from under the roof, scraping my arm on a nail. I was bleeding badly but I had no time to take care of the wound.

After running for an hour and a half, I came to the house of a forester who was a friend of the Koelewyns, and I begged him to let me in. When he saw that I was hurt, he called a doctor who knew I was Jewish but came to the house to stitch my arm anyway.

Meanwhile the forester, who had a wife and child, said it was too dangerous for him to hide me. I became very fright-ened that I had no place to go.

But he managed to get word to the Koelewyns, and they contacted Uncle Willem. Two days later the woman who was hiding my parents came for me and took me to her house in Amsterdam. When I saw my mother and father, I didn't want to leave them. But Amsterdam was much too unsafe for a Jewish child. Not long after a young man from the underground came for me.

This man took me by ferryboat over the Zuider Zee to a province called Friesland in northern Holland. It was now October 1943, and Jews were officially prohibited from be-ing in the open. If we had been caught, it would have been the end for both of us.

In Friesland I was brought to a family whose last name

was Bootsma. The parents were elderly, in their sixties, and owned a bakery in a tiny village. They had nine grown children, and the two youngest sons, Roelof, twenty-six, and Harm, twenty-one, lived at home.

From the beginning I became attached to Harm. As soon as he saw how confused and frightened I was, he went out of his way to make me feel better. We shared a room, and like a big brother, he joked with me and also talked kindly. When he delivered bread in his covered horse-drawn carriage, he took me along with him.

To protect me, the Dutch underground had forged totally new identity papers that said I was a Christian child who had lost his parents in the city bombings. The Bootsmas pretended to be taking me in to raise me as part of their family.

I called the couple ''Heit'' and ''Mem,'' which meant ''Daddy'' and ''Mommy'' in their dialect. Since I was supposed to be Christian, I went to church with them on Sundays and studied the Bible. During the week I attended school like every other Dutch child in the community.

It didn't take long for me to make friends. Every Saturday I went with a group of kids to the lake, and we'd all swim in our underwear.

It was a happy year. After school and on vacation I worked in the bakery, where Heit, in his fatherly way, showed me how to prepare the dough for bread. I loved this job.

Heit was affectionate and so was Mem, who acted like a real mother, making sure I took my weekly bath. With the two of them and Harm, I felt comfortable and safe.

But one day in the fall of 1944, a Jewish family in the village and the people who were hiding them were suddenly

*Mem Bootsma and Heit Bootsma.*

arrested by the Germans. Word soon spread that there were collaborators in the Dutch police. Everyone was scared, because throughout Friesland there were numerous Jewish children staying with Gentiles. The first thing the Bootsmas did was take me out of school and keep me close by.

At this same time, the Germans started making unexpected visits to Dutch homes, rounding up young men for slave labor. One Sunday in church the door was flung open and someone screamed, ''Germans coming!'' All the young guys ran out to hide.

The Bootsmas were worried for their sons and for me, and they built a special hiding place for us under the living room floor. Whenever we sensed danger, we lifted up the wooden floor panels and climbed down. Mostly I stayed there by myself, but sometimes if Harm or other young men were in the house, we hid together.

While the Germans searched we'd play chess and laugh quietly with one another. But I was always frightened, especially when I was alone. Through the wall grating I could see German soldiers standing outside and was petrified they might see me too.

Up until then nobody had questioned my dark hair, which was very unusual among typically blond Christian Dutch children. With the Germans in the area, though, it was too dangerous for me to walk around that way. So every week Mem took me to the barber to have my hair dyed. Instead of coming out blond, it turned out red. I looked funny, but I didn't care. I would have done anything to survive.

Meanwhile the Germans began hunting for Jews and Dutch men in the middle of the night. If they came to our house, I could never get under the living room floor in time, since my bedroom was in the attic. So the Bootsmas built a false wall between my closet and the room next to it, making a space big enough for one person to stand or sit in.

Several times I hid there while German soldiers tramped through. For hours I'd be in the dark with nothing to do. I was so scared, I'd start to weep. More than once I soiled my pants. I also began to wet my bed even though I was twelve years old.

Every moment I was in terror. Even during the day when I hung around the bakery I could never relax. Once the Germans surprised us there, and I had to race into the barn and hide behind a pile of wood we kept to heat the oven. Suddenly I noticed another boy hiding behind the wood too.

Neither of us said a word, but we each knew the other's story.

Right about this time, the underground warned us that there might be more collaborators in the Dutch police than they first suspected. They said there'd be an increase in night raids and that we should take extra precautions. Instead of sleeping in the house, I stayed with different farmers, hiding in haylofts.

Then that became unsafe, and I spent the next few months sleeping on a small barge belonging to the Bootsmas' daughter and son-in-law. The boat was on a lake near a canal, about a half mile from our house. It wasn't that far away, but to me it seemed like a tremendous distance, especially after I got scabies all over my body and was alone at night feeling miserable.

That September southern Holland was liberated, but the Germans still occupied the northern part where we were. For months and months, while the Germans were entrenched there, people in the cities were dying of famine. And the winter was an unusually cold one. It was freezing on the barge.

By March the Germans were on the waters too, so I had to find another hiding place. This time I slept in haystacks near the farmhouses of people the Bootsmas knew and ate whatever the farmers would give me. I kept thinking, How much longer can this go on?

Then, one day in April 1945, a man on a bike rode past the farm where I was and yelled, "We are liberated!" I was so excited, I ran through the fields and leaped from one small canal to another until I found the Canadian soldiers who had freed our town. They looked magnificent in their uniforms.

Afterward I went back to the Bootsmas' house. Less than a month later, when Amsterdam was freed, my father arrived. He said he was with the Dutch underground and he carried a gun. I was very impressed with that gun and the chocolates he had brought for me.

Now it was time for me to return to my parents. I had great difficulty saying good-bye to the Bootsmas, and they didn't part easily from me. But luckily that was not the end of our relationship. I saw them a couple of times a year until they died in the 1950s.

The Bootsmas were my war parents, and Harm was like a brother to me. I'll never forget that family. They did everything to help me survive.

POSTSCRIPT

I lived in Holland until 1988, and all that time I kept in close contact with Harm. I still see him because I have an apartment in Amsterdam and we visit together frequently.

Through the years Harm and I have talked about why his family hid me. He says they did what they believed in, and if the identical situation arose today he's positive they'd make the same decision. He told me they knew the penalties if they were caught, but that was not as important to them as saving a Jewish child's life.

In Holland only 20 percent of the Jewish population survived the war. More than four thousand of the survivors were children hidden by Gentiles. I was one of the lucky ones.

*Jacques in 1993.*

The Israeli ambassador personally gave Harm a medal and certificate posthumously honoring his parents at Yad Vashem, and Harm too got recognition at Yad Vashem. Although Jacques didn't know this until after the war, Harm had been in the underground and had saved the lives of many Jewish people.

*Jacques is retired. He had been an agent for textile mills.*

71

*Sylvia Richter, age 9, with her mother and brother, Danny.*

# SYLVIA RICHTER

POLAND

*"The situation was grim, but being
close to my family made me feel safe"*

I grew up in Poland, in a house that my family owned. It was next to a park and on the same block as the shul. Every Saturday my father took me to synagogue, and while he prayed, I stared in awe at the silver Torah cases and the shiny ornaments.

In 1941 the Germans bombed our town and SS men robbed us of our silver and valuable fabrics. Because we had the reputation of being rich, an important SS official stationed himself at our home. I was terrified of him. He'd eat at the dinner table with us and smile at me, but I was too frightened to smile back.

Meanwhile, from our terrace, my younger brother Danny and I watched Germans herd Jews from other towns into our synagogue. Later we'd see them shipping them out. One hot summer day when I was four, my father without explanation dressed me in my baggy winter leggings. He filled them with chunks of bread, and carried me to shul. There he walked up and down the aisle, handing out bread to whimpering people. I was amazed how different the synagogue looked. The Germans had stripped it of its silver and Oriental rugs.

Soon after, my father was beaten by the SS for refusing to obey an order. When he recovered, we all left in the night for my grandparents' town. But the situation for Jews wasn't any better there, so for the next year my family, with my maternal grandparents and two aunts and two uncles, went from village to village, thinking maybe in the remote areas we'd be safer.

Since my father had been active in town affairs, he knew a lot of Gentiles, including the mayor. Wherever we went, he and my uncles contacted people who helped us hide in barns, stables, and a basement warehouse. Each place was more dangerous than the last. During this time my grandmother became sick and died.

In September 1943, when I was six, my Uncle Srulka approached a former business acquaintance of his and asked if he could protect us. This man, Mr. Plotkowski, said we all could stay in the hayloft above the stable where he kept his animals. That became our new home.

The hayloft was very long and low, so we couldn't stand up in it. During the day we mostly lay in the straw, but at night we crawled into a tiny thatch shelter that Mr. Plotkowski had partitioned off from the rest of the area. He felt we'd be safer sleeping there. He gave us one sheet, a pillow, and a down comforter, and he also supplied us with a jug of water and a chamber pot that the adults emptied at night. It was very cramped in that little room.

Meanwhile Mrs. Plotkowski prepared our food, but she and their two young children, who were ten and twelve, never came up to the hayloft. In fact the children had no idea we were there. Only Mr. Plotkowski and their twenty-year-old son, Jan, visited, slipping us something to eat when they fed their dog, Bobchio.

Bobchio was chained to the barn entrance. If a stranger walked by the barn, he'd perk up his ears and bark, alerting us to crawl quickly into our room. He was Danny's and my friend and our main source of entertainment.

The rest of the hours my father taught us Hebrew prayers and Polish poems, and my aunt and mother told us fairy tales. Everything was done in a whisper.

From the beginning, food was scarce. Mr. Plotkowski could not feed us all, so at night the grown-ups foraged at neighboring farms or pleaded with Gentiles they knew to give us whatever they could. Once in a while they came back with a little piece of cheese or some milk, but we still were always hungry.

Soon after we arrived, there were rumors that the Germans were intensifying their search for Jews. Mr. Plotkowski told us to leave the barn and directed us to a deep underground ditch, where we lay in the dirt for almost a week. After that the adults decided that we would be safer if the family split up.

My parents, Danny, and I stayed with the Plotkowskis, and the rest of my relatives went to hide on a nearby farm owned by another Gentile my uncle knew. At night my father joined them when they scrounged for food. Other evenings they'd come to visit us and we'd all huddle in our shelter. I loved snuggling up with my aunt, and Danny liked lying in our grandfather's arms. The situation was grim, but being close to my family made me feel safe.

In November it turned very cold, and four feet of snow

covered the ground. Jan gave us cornhusks to insulate the thatched walls of the shelter, but we were still freezing. And we were infested with lice. I couldn't stop whimpering.

Danny, who was just four, wasn't happy either. Day and night he cried loudly for milk and bread and butter. Quickly my father would put his hand over Danny's mouth to quiet him, but that only made Danny cry more.

One night in mid-December Mr. Plotkowski suddenly appeared in the hayloft with his wife. It was the first time she had come to see us, and she was in a panic. She said there were more rumors about Germans searching homes and barns for Jews, and she was terrified that her family would be caught. She already knew about one Polish family who had been found hiding Jews; the Germans burned their barn with all the animals in it, shot the children, and killed the couple.

Now the Germans were saying that all Jews had to be out of the area by Christmas. Mr. and Mrs. Plotkowski told us that we couldn't stay with them anymore and to make plans to leave soon.

That night my father went to talk to my uncles to see if they could help. He wasn't back by morning. The next evening he still didn't return. We were petrified. Two weeks later, Mr. Plotkowski came up to the hayloft and told Danny and me to go into the little room. ''I want to speak to your mother,'' he said.

Through the thatched wall I could hear him crying. When he finally left, I saw that my mother was very upset. I knew something terrible had happened. My mother told Danny and me that our father and uncle had been found dead. For the first time in hiding, I cried aloud.

It took almost two months for us to get over the shock. Day and night we lay next to one another in the shelter, pressing our bodies close together for comfort.

All this time our relatives didn't visit. Only Jan and Mr. Plotkowski came up to bring us food. Neither mentioned another word about us having to go.

By the end of February, when we felt a little better, Danny and I crawled out of the shelter and lay in the hayloft again to spend a few minutes watching the dog. Once Danny leaned over too far and landed right in front of Bobchio's feet. I was scared that Bobchio would bark and attract attention. But he just looked at Danny and wagged his tail.

March 14 was my seventh birthday. By then we had been in the hayloft for six months. That morning my mother told me she had a surprise. She pointed to a hole the size of a quarter that she had made in the outside wall. "It's your birthday present," she said, "a tiny window to the world."

That same day a bird came to the hole and put his beak through. "The bird is coming with good news, like the dove who came to Noah," my mother said, and she told Danny and me the Bible story. She compared our hiding place to the ark and said, "We have violent waters and danger around us. But like Noah, we are safe inside."

Now that my father was gone, Mr. Plotkowski came to see us more often. He would bring flyers that had fallen from Russian and German planes and give them to my mother so she'd know what was going on in the world. When she finished reading them, she made them into paper hats and planes for Danny and me to play with. She also showed us how to braid straw so we could make baskets.

One time Mr. Plotkowski went to the town garbage dump

and found a page from a Hebrew book. He wrapped it carefully in a leaf so no one could see what it was and later gave it to my mother. From that piece of paper she taught us the Hebrew alphabet, pointing to each letter. *Yod:* "This letter is very small, like the Jewish people," she said, "but it is very important."

Meanwhile we were still in tremendous danger, with anti-Semitic Ukrainians and Germans swarming everywhere. Sometimes it was too dangerous for Mr. Plotkowski to bring us our food and water. Once I was watching him carry bread under his arm for us, when he suddenly threw it to the dog. Afterward he told us he had seen a stranger approaching and had gotten scared. Another time he was walking with a bowl of sauce when a squirrel ran by and startled him. In fright, he dropped the dish.

On the nights that he didn't come, we were starving. My mother tried to comfort us by taking out a gold chain she kept hidden in her bra and pointing to the links. "These are worth a lot of money," she said to Danny and me. "Some day we'll be able to buy all the bread we want."

But Danny and I wanted food now. So my mother would climb down from the hayloft and sneak over to a nearby farm to pick whatever she could find. One night she didn't come back when she was supposed to, and Danny and I thought she must have been killed. We held onto each other, whimpering, until she finally appeared. Two teenagers had been making love near the barn, and she had to wait until they were gone.

When the weather became warmer, I looked through the hole and saw Polish children playing hide-and-go-seek.

Danny and I played hide-and-go-seek too, in the hay, but we couldn't run around and make noise. I'd ask my brother, "If you had a choice, what kind of animal would you like to be?" Sometimes he'd choose a lion because it was strong and protected people. Another time he'd say an elephant. But I always wanted to be a bird. That way I'd be free to fly away from the hayloft.

By now the Germans, with the help of Ukrainians, were searching furiously for Jews. More than once they climbed up to the hayloft and jabbed the straw with their bayonets. We'd sit in the shelter holding our breath until they were gone.

Then, in the middle of one night, Ukrainians came with a German shepherd. Suddenly they let the dog off the leash, and just as the dog was about to dash up to the hayloft, Bobchio attacked. When Mr. Plotkowski heard the noise, he came running, in time to prevent the Ukrainians from shooting Bobchio.

Mr. Plotkowski explained that he needed Bobchio to protect his livestock and offered to personally escort the Ukrainians to the hayloft while their dog stayed below.

As the Ukrainians flashed their lights through the shelter wall, Danny and I clung to our mother. We didn't make a sound until the men left.

That May Mr. Plotkowski was sent to a German labor camp. About three weeks later Mrs. Plotkowski came to tell us that the Russians had liberated our area. "You are free," she said. But my mother was afraid to go into the open. In February and March there had been false rumors that the war had ended, and when Jews came out of hiding, they were shot by the Ukrainians. We didn't leave at that time because there was snow on the ground and we had no boots. Now my mother wasn't taking chances until she was positive that things were safe.

She also wanted to wait until our relatives found us. In the meantime Mrs. Plotkowski took our clothes and bedding to wash, and she gave us soap and water to clean ourselves. She gave my mother a comb to delouse our hair.

After three weeks my mother was convinced we were really free. Still there was no news from our family. With each day she felt less hope. Finally she told Danny and me that all of them must have died and that there was no need for us to stay any longer. I couldn't stop crying.

And I worried that without Mr. Plotkowski there'd be no one to tell us what to do. We didn't even know how to get to the main road. Mrs. Plotkowski said that Jan would show us the way. But we had to be careful because Ukrainians who had collaborated with the Germans might shoot us. She gave my mother a kerchief to wear so she'd look like a Polish woman, and my mother braided my hair to make me look like a Polish child.

Finally it was time to leave. Slowly we crawled out of the shelter, and then Mrs. Plotkowski helped us climb down from the hayloft. After nine months of crouching we couldn't stand up straight and could barely walk. Also, because we had spoken in a whisper for so long, Danny and I had forgotten how to talk in a normal voice.

First Danny and I said good-bye to Bobchio and thanked him for saving our lives. Then we thanked Mrs. Plotkowski. She said to my mother, "Never tell anyone that we hid you or anti-Jewish villagers might kill us.'' And Jan made my mother promise not to get in touch with his family again.

Before we left, my mother pointed out two trees, one on either side of the barn. ''That's a good way to remember this place,'' she said to Danny and me.

Jan led us to the main road and eventually we made our way to a displaced persons' camp. We lived there for the next two years until we sailed to the United States. In time my mother was remarried, to a man who was like another father to me. He was such a decent person, I'm sure that my own father would have selected him to take his place.

My mother never contacted the Plotkowskis again, and often she told me how sad this made her. But she would not break her promise to them. All she could do was keep their memory alive in Danny and me.

*Sylvia in 1993.*

POSTSCRIPT

In 1990, fifteen years after my mother had died, Poland was no longer controlled by Russia, so I went back there to see if I could find the Plotkowskis. I wanted to ask them if they were ready to reveal that they had hidden Jews.

The Plotkowskis' farmhouse had become a school, and the barn was no longer there. But the two trees my mother had pointed out were still standing.

From neighbors I learned that shortly after the war the Plotkowskis had moved to another village, and that both Mr. and Mrs. Plotkowski had died. But Jan was alive and in his sixties. When I got back to the United States, I wrote to him and he answered me. He wanted to know if I was the Jew who had been hidden in the hayloft or one of those who had stayed in the chimney. I hadn't even known there were others hidden besides my family.

In 1991 Jan came to America to attend a conference for hidden children and their rescuers. He stayed at my house for two weeks, and in Polish I told him how I felt about his family.

I said that his father was an angel who had superhuman compassion for people, and his mother was a good person too. At first she wanted to send us away to protect her own family, but in the end she knew she'd be shipping us to our death. "And you, Jan," I said, "you have a heart of gold."

*Mr. Plotkowski's name is listed in Yad Vashem as a righteous rescuer. Sylvia is a teacher and gives talks about her war experience.*

*Jan Plotkowski in 1991 with Sylvia's grandsons.*

*Andy Sterling, age 6, in 1942, with his mother
and sister, Judith.*

# ANDY STERLING

*"It was the first time I was on my own"*

In 1941 Hungary, where I was born, entered the war as a German ally. A year later, when I was six and a half, my father and other Jewish men in our village were sent away to do forced labor. For the next eighteen months I didn't know where he was.

When he came back in late 1943, he told my family stories about Jews being rounded up throughout Europe and said that we were no longer safe. He thought we should leave our small village of Nagykata where everyone knew we were Jewish and go to Budapest, the capital city, where we might blend in more.

First my parents left and moved in with my aunt. For the next few months they tried to get things in order. Suddenly, in March 1944, the Germans occupied Hungary, and Jews living in and near my village were relocated to a ghetto. My grandmother, my younger sister, Judith, and I went there along with my grandmother's brother and his wife.

Every day Jews from this ghetto were being sent to the camps. We knew that our time was running out. Luckily my uncle's daughter knew a Christian who had connections and helped us to escape. A few weeks later we learned that all the Jews in our ghetto had been shipped to Auschwitz.

Now I was with my parents again. My father had already gotten false identity papers for himself and had become an ambulance driver. I, though, had to wear a star and abide by the curfew.

That September the Germans, with the Hungarian SS as their helpers, began deporting Jews in huge numbers and shooting Jews on the street. At the same time, the Russians were bombing the city. Things got so bad, my parents forbade me to leave the apartment and said I could play only in the garden within the building.

One day I disobeyed and went across the street with a little mirror to see how the sun's rays reflected off it. Out of nowhere, an SS man holding a leashed German shepherd appeared and grabbed me by the collar. He accused me of giving signals to American flyers and was about to take me away when the superintendent of my apartment house came to my rescue. He convinced the SS man to let me go.

At this point my parents realized how much danger we were in and said that my sister and I had to be hidden. When I heard that I'd be separated from my parents, I was very upset.

My parents said I'd be going to a Catholic orphanage in Budapest with Paul, their friend's child, who was two years older than I. Paul's parents had found the place, and the priest in charge was willing to hide us. Judith, now five, was being sent to a convent, and my mother was going to live with a Catholic family in town. My father said he'd be moving around in his ambulance trying to get false papers for my aunt and grandmother.

Before I left, my parents warned me not to tell anyone at the orphanage I was Jewish. Because I was circumcised, they said I had to be extra careful not to be seen when I undressed or urinated.

In October 1944 my father drove Paul and me to the orphanage. We left at night in the middle of an air raid, when only emergency vehicles were allowed on the street.

As soon as we got to the door, my father said good-bye and promised to visit whenever he could. As he drove away, I felt abandoned. It was the first time I was on my own.

The priest and his assistant took Paul and me into an office and told us never to talk about being Jewish, not even to each other. If the orphanage boys asked why we had come a month after school had started, we were to say that our fathers had been killed on the front and that our mothers were too ill to take care of us.

After the priest coached us on some of the morning prayers, he showed us to the dormitory. I lay in bed terrified. Everything was strange. I wanted my parents.

The next morning the priest introduced us to the boys. There were sixty of them, and most had been in the orphanage for years and years and knew one another. I had only met Paul twice before.

That morning I went to services and carefully watched what the others did. When they stood up, I stood up. When they knelt, I knelt. But when they crossed themselves, I got uncomfortable. I had been brought up in a Jewish home and gone to Hebrew school, and I felt awkward. In the end I crossed myself like the rest of the boys, and from then on I did what I was told. I was too afraid to do anything else.

My father visited from time to time. He could only stay

for a few minutes, but at least I knew he was alive. Once in a while he came when I wasn't around, and the priest would give me the message. The priest tried to look after me and make sure I was okay, but with so many boys to take care of he didn't always have the time. Mostly I fended for myself.

In November, one month after I arrived, the bombing increased and the air raid sirens went off night and day. In a hurry we'd all rush down into the bunker, where the priest would lead us in prayer. In between the bombings the priest and his assistant tried to conduct classes, but when the air raids became too frequent, they gave up.

After that we moved into the bunker full time, running upstairs only to use the bathroom. We'd go in shifts of four or five, with just twenty-five seconds each. For emergencies we kept some buckets downstairs.

By then it was winter, and it was very cold. We had no heat or electricity, and there was a water shortage. That meant we couldn't bathe or change our clothes. For me it was easier not having to undress in front of the others. But soon we all were infested with lice.

At this time the Russians invaded Budapest, arriving in tanks. They destroyed one building after another until the Germans and the Hungarian SS were trapped and resorted to street fighting. It got so dangerous, my father was afraid to drive his ambulance and stopped coming to see me. Now I felt totally alone.

Worse, we were running out of food. Except for some corn left in the pantry, there was nothing to eat. In desperation the priest ran out on the street to scrounge up something. Once he found a dead horse that had been shot in front of the orphanage and asked me and some other boys to help chop it up. That night he grilled the meat over some wood, and everyone had a couple of bites. The meat tasted sweet. After not eating for so long, I thought it was an incredible meal.

By late December the bombing had worsened, and fires were spreading throughout the city. When a building to the right of ours was shelled, the priest got scared. He thought the Russians were probably targeting the Hungarian Gestapo's headquarters, which were next to the orphanage. To protect us, he decided to break through the wall of our cellar and tunnel into the adjacent building where it would be safer.

With only a pickax, he and his assistant chipped away at the bunker's stone wall, shoveling out the debris. Meanwhile bombs and shells whistled overhead. We kids watched, petrified. Eventually they dug out a large enough space for us to crawl through one at a time.

By then I hadn't seen my father in a month and a half. I didn't know where he or my mother were or if they were alive or dead. It was tough not having any word from them.

At the same time the firing outside was getting more severe. The older boys in the orphanage tried to act brave, but the younger ones, like Paul and me, couldn't stop crying. He and I clung to each other while the priest kept telling us to pray.

"The war is almost over," the priest said to everyone. With the bombing overhead, it was hard to believe, especially since the priest himself seemed scared. Only when he said I'd soon be with my parents did I have some hope.

Finally, on January 15, 1945, the Russians liberated Pest, the part of the city where I was hiding. With the priest leading us, we all went into the street to witness the events. Except for some distant shelling in the hills, it was deadly silent. I looked around and saw one building after another in rubble. Suddenly my whole body started shaking. Instead of feeling joy, I felt weak. More than ever I wanted my parents.

Six days later my father drove up in his ambulance. When I saw him, I ran into his arms and couldn't stop crying. He had brought bread for everyone, which we quickly grabbed. We were very hungry.

Now, I thought, I'll finally be with my parents. But Buda, the part of the city where my mother was hiding, hadn't yet been liberated. My father didn't even know if she was safe. Also, there were still pockets of Germans around who were shooting at whim, so I had to stay in the orphanage for another two months.

During that time my father visited and brought everyone food. Then in March he came for me, taking me to my aunt's apartment, where once again the family was together. The four of us and my aunt and grandmother had survived the war.

Now we had to figure out how to get food and clothing to keep us alive. Since my father had to give the ambulance back to the government, we had no transportation. Besides, there was nothing to be bought in the city. So my parents walked forty miles back to our old village to see what they could find there. A week later they returned in a donkey cart filled with enough food for us and extra to sell. Not long after, we all left Budapest and returned to our home in Nagykata.

Of the 628 Jews who had lived in and around our village, very few had survived the war. When the villagers saw us, they acted as if we had returned from the dead.

In school, my sister and I were the only Jewish children in our classes, which made us feel strange. My parents too were uncomfortable with no other Jews nearby. So in 1949 we moved back to Budapest. Until the year before, my father had been sending donations to the orphanage. But then in 1948 the Communists banned religious schools in the country, and the orphanage ceased to exist. The building was standing, but the priest, his assistant, and the children were gone.

I never saw the priest again, but I learned from my father that there were eight other Jewish boys in the orphanage besides Paul and me. Paul and I had suspected certain kids were Jewish, but we had been afraid to ask. It's too bad, because it would have been comforting to know we weren't the only ones.

*Andy in 1993.*

POSTSCRIPT

The older I got, the more I realized what a courageous man the priest was. He took in Jewish kids not because the pope dictated it, but because he thought it was morally right to save a life. He was a saintly person.

In 1956 my family escaped from Communist Hungary and came to America. Two years ago, when Hungary became a free country again, I went back for a visit and saw the orphanage building. It looked the same, but the religious feeling was gone.

Still, I knew that those five months I lived with the priest had played a major role in my life. I learned from him what it means to give, and today I try to lead that kind of life. The priest was a truly wonderful person. I'm thankful to have been in his care.

*Andy is a construction engineer.*

*Hirsch Grunstein, age 14, in 1942.*

# HIRSCH GRUNSTEIN

BELGIUM

## *"I hated being locked up"*

For the first two years of my life I lived in Poland. Then my family moved to Antwerp, Belgium, where my father was in the diamond business. We were very religious. We didn't travel or turn on lights on the Sabbath, and I always kept my head covered, Yet I went to a state high school, where I was called "Henri."

As I was growing up, my parents talked about why we had left Poland. They said it was dangerous for us there, because the police did not protect the Jews. Yet my parents didn't seem to mind that in Belgium there were signs saying JEWS DON'T APPLY HERE FOR APARTMENTS. They felt this country was safe. Then in 1940 the Germans invaded. I was twelve at the time, and my brother Salomon was six and a half.

Within two years Jews weren't allowed on the street, and there was a rumor that Jews were being sent back to their country of origin. When my mother heard this, she cried, "Go back to Poland? We might as well throw ourselves into the river."

That's when she and my father decided to hide my brother and me. She spoke to a friend whose two young sons were already with the Van Dammes, a Gentile couple in a small village. The couple's daughter, Alice, had made the arrangements and had now convinced her brother, Gaston, and his wife, Adrienne, to hide Jewish children too.

Gaston and Adrienne were in their twenties and were hoping to get very young children. When Adrienne came with Alice to meet us, she was disappointed to see how old we were. Yet she and Gaston decided to take us in anyhow, thinking the war would be over soon and our stay would be short.

Meanwhile my father was saying that maybe our family should escape to Switzerland. He told Adrienne that if we came to live with her, we'd arrive unannounced on a Saturday, the day Belgians dressed up and visited one another.

By the end of the week my father had contacted my former schoolteacher, René Govaerts, who was helping to hide Jews. He asked Govaerts to take us to Adrienne and Gaston's house on the Friday night of Rosh Hashanah, the Jewish New Year, when we'd ordinarily never travel. My father said that if we were going to play Aryan, we might as well do it all the way. He even told my brother and me not to cover our heads anymore. And he changed our last name to "Govaerts" to sound Gentile, while Salomon became "Sylvain," and I kept "Henri."

My father packed one tiny suitcase for both of us so we wouldn't attract attention. In it he put a little prayer book and the Book of Psalms. "If Mama and I don't survive, I want you to teach your brother about Judaism," he said. He also made me memorize the address of my uncle in America in case I needed to get in touch with him after the war.

It was hard leaving my parents. I worried, now that the Germans were searching door to door for Jews. My father tried to reassure me that they'd be fine. My mother, though, was too upset to talk.

We left after curfew when it was dark and quiet on the street. I was sure everyone could hear the noise the metal taps on my shoes made. As we rode the dimly lit tram to Govaerts' home in the suburbs, my heart pounded. I couldn't wait to get this whole thing over with.

At ten the next morning we arrived at Adrienne's house and surprised her as she was busily scrubbing her patio. Later Gaston came home and was happy to see us. He and Adrienne gave us their room with the big bed, while they moved into a smaller one. They wanted us to be comfortable and did whatever they could to cheer us up, even staging wrestling matches on the kitchen floor. But Salomon and I were very sad. We missed our parents.

From the beginning I felt responsible for reminding Salomon he was a Jew and insisted that he pray every day. But he wanted to play with the village kids, while I read books and took long walks. Soon he was speaking the local Flemish dialect and wearing wooden shoes and peasant clothing like a native.

Two weeks after we arrived, my parents suddenly appeared. They were going to be staying close by, with Adrienne's parents. At first I was thrilled to have them near, but then I realized this wasn't a good arrangement. Because they had heavy Polish accents, they couldn't move about freely, so visiting them was like seeing people in jail. Also, Salomon and I were running to Adrienne's parents' house too often, and Adrienne was afraid the villagers might become suspicious. So my parents went to live with her sister in another town.

By the middle of October, it was obvious the war was not ending quickly. As city kids supposedly on a short vacation, Salomon and I should have been returning home, especially since the local children my age were already in school or taking up a trade. When I asked Gaston if I could help him and his father in their blacksmith shop, he said he didn't want me around the glowing hot irons.

Meanwhile he and Adrienne had already told the villagers that Salomon was staying with them longer because he was sickly and needed fresh country air. But they couldn't think of an excuse for my being there. So they said I should stay indoors and keep out of sight.

Now that Salomon and I were going to be around for a while, Adrienne and Gaston reclaimed their bedroom. Since I had to be inside, they let me use it during the day because it was large and had a window. If I stood in the shadows, I could watch the people on the street.

Other than that there wasn't much for me to do. After I said my morning prayers, read the newspaper, and ate the meals that Adrienne brought up for me, I was very bored. I knew that all my Gentile friends in Antwerp had started their third year of Latin and algebra and thought maybe I should teach myself those subjects. When Govaerts came to visit Adrienne and Gaston (they had become friends), I asked him to bring me some textbooks. But as soon as I took one look at the books, I put them aside for another day, thinking I had plenty of time to study.

Next I tried to make a drawing of the bedroom to keep as a record of my hiding experience, but when it didn't come out right, I gave that up. I also played solitaire and built castles with decks of cards, but still there were hours I was by myself with nothing to do.

When winter arrived, I was allowed downstairs for dinner, because it got dark early and neighbors were less likely to stop by. Also, on stormy afternoons Adrienne would call me to the kitchen to have coffee and cookies with her. She always locked the door beforehand so no one could surprise us.

With the cold weather the house was freezing, especially in the morning. To keep my blood circulating and to warm my body, I rubbed my hands and legs and swung them back and forth. Soon I made this my daily exercise program and filled up more time by reading magazines and short novels that Adrienne and Gaston gave me. Still, I felt lost. And I was angry. Just because I was Jewish, the Germans weren't letting me lead a normal life.

In late spring, it was even harder for me. Through the open bedroom window I sometimes heard music and saw people going to the cafes or for a walk. I had just turned fifteen, and I too wanted to be free to come and go. Instead I was in my own private prison. Other than the cat, there was no one to keep me company. Sometimes Salomon came up, but he was five and a half years younger than I, and we didn't share the same interests.

Each day I became more and more furious. I'd read the ritual prayers, wanting to hear about a God who would sock it to the Germans, but that wasn't the kind I was finding. Although I knew that there were periods in history when Jews suffered, I wondered, Why is this happening to me? Sometimes I'd remember Bible passages with the phrase "because of your sins" and think maybe I was being punished for having torn paper on the Sabbath. For spite, I'd rip up paper to see what might occur.

Then one day I opened the Hebrew Book of Psalms that my father had slipped into the suitcase. I wasn't even sure what I was looking for. Suddenly I came upon phrases like "smite the enemy" and "shatter them to pieces." The words startled me. They had been written thousands of years ago, and yet they seemed to be directed at the Germans. For the first time in months, I was excited. I felt a connection in time and space to the Jewish people.

I couldn't wait to read more of the Psalms and made them my reward for the day. I'd rush through my morning prayers, do my exercise, and read the newspaper, building up energy toward the Psalms. The words were so gripping, I felt as though I was being transported to another world. One day I could almost taste and feel the desert of Israel; another, I witnessed earthquakes and fire devouring the enemy.

When I got to Paslm 23, "The Lord Is My Shepherd," I read in Hebrew, "I shall not be afraid of harm." At that moment I began to have hope.

Around this time Gaston gave me a book titled *Automobile Course,* written by an engineer. As a blacksmith, Gaston knew that the days of the horse and wagon were numbered, and he thought I would be interested in what the future might bring. Although the book was very thin, it carefully detailed how a car worked, starting with the very first raw explosion within the engine to the car's being thrust into motion. I was fascinated. Then and there in my isolated room I decided to become an engineer and an inventor.

While a large part of my day was filled with learning, I still had the late afternoon and evening to occupy myself, especially in summer, when it got dark late. During those hours I'd fantasize confrontations with the Germans in which I always came out the victor.

I also daydreamed what it would be like if I were the only Jew left after the war. The thought terrified me. I didn't want such a burden. I decided I'd run away to Norway, pretend I was a Christian, then stroll through the streets with beautiful women. The nearer I approached my sixteenth birthday, the more I wanted to be with girls. I was furious that I wasn't able to. I hated being locked up.

Occasionally on a holiday or a Sunday Adrienne and Gaston told people that I had come for a short visit, having arrived from the city on the night train. In the morning the villagers would see me in my best clothes, acting very well behaved. On Sunday I was sent to church, even though Adrienne and Gaston rarely attended. They didn't want people to wonder. I'd sit in the back, terrified, as I mouthed the prayers.

On some of these "visits," Adrienne took Salomon and me to see our parents. Although I was happy being with them, the get-togethers were always sad. Instead of the four of us sitting down to dinner like a real family, I felt more like a guest who had to leave at a certain hour.

Meanwhile Salomon had learned how to move among the villagers without arousing the slightest suspicion. Whenever he got into a fight with another child, he was the first to throw the insult, "You Jew!"

One time he was on the road when the priest came by,

leading a procession through the village. Salomon saw the people go down on one knee and cross themselves, and he did the same. Later he came home all excited and proudly told Adrienne what had happened. From my room upstairs I overheard Adrienne say, "You did just fine."

At night when he crawled into bed, I yelled, "You're a Jewish boy! Couldn't you have run somewhere?"

Salomon was confused. The next morning he asked Adrienne if he had done something wrong. Adrienne replied in a voice loud enough for me to hear, "You did the right thing, Sylvain."

I felt defeated, especially when Gaston too praised Salomon for thinking so quickly. Gaston said that by acting like a Christian, my brother had protected himself. But then he added, "You know, as a Jewish boy you don't have to say the prayers when you kneel and cross yourself. Instead, you can say . . ." and he came out with one of the worst Flemish curses. I couldn't stop laughing. Adrienne, who usually jumped on him for bad language, didn't this time.

Until this time our village had never been bothered by the Germans. But one day in April of 1944 they captured a courier from the underground and found him with a list of Jewish children being hidden. From the list, the Germans learned about the two young boys who were staying with Gaston's parents and came to get them. Gaston, who had been in the house, ran for the fields under a hail of bullets.

The Germans then came looking for him at our house. When Adrienne said she didn't know where he was, they arrested her and me. Salomon, who had been watching all this from the street, hid in the field until dark, and then he went to Adrienne's mother's house.

The Germans took all of us on the list to a temporary shelter for children until we could be deported. They didn't know that the Belgian underground was helping us there, making sure we had enough food while they planned for our escape. Oddly, at the shelter I felt more free than at Adrienne and Gaston's house. At least I was with Jewish kids my age. Still, I was petrified that at any moment the German police would surround the place and take us away.

Four months later, just two days before the Germans were to deport us, the Belgian underground got us out of the shelter and brought us to a little village. Soon after, Belgium was liberated, and within a few days my parents found me. We returned to Antwerp and waited to hear news about Adrienne. The day she was let out of the concentration camp, I went to visit her.

From then on our families saw one another regularly, and we were very close. Adrienne and Gaston were at my brother's Bar Mitzvah. And when they had a son, they gave him Salomon's war name, Sylvain.

Meanwhile, they told the villagers that Salomon and I were Jewish. The villagers refused to believe them. They thought Adrienne and Gaston had made it up because it had become fashionable to say you had hidden Jews during the war.

In 1958 I moved to the United States but the rest of my family remained in Belgium. Whenever I went to visit them, about four or five times a year, I always went to see Adrienne and Gaston.

I never asked why they took Salomon and me in. Maybe it's because they loved children and were willing to take a big risk to protect them. The longer we were together, the more attached we became.

Often my mother and I talked about them. She said she wasn't sure if she could have hidden even her own relatives. We both agreed that Adrienne and Gaston were truly remarkable people. They acted from the heart and never complained or seemed regretful. They made Salomon and me feel we were at home. From the moment I started living with them, they became my other family. I love them. I really do.

POSTSCRIPT

A few years ago both of my parents died. Adrienne and Gaston said to me, "As long as we're alive, you'll have another home." I knew they meant it.

In March 1993, both Adrienne and Gaston turned eighty. I was with them on their fiftieth wedding anniversary, and I also was there at the birthday celebration. My daughter, Eva, and Salomon and his daughter and son-in-law came too.

*Hirsch in 1993.*

At the banquet, which twenty-five family members attended, Gaston, Adrienne, and Gaston's sister Alice were honored for rescuing Jews. Two members of Le Consistoire Central Israelite de Belgique personally gave them each a medal and certificate in the name of the entire Jewish-Belgian community. It was a day none of us will forget.

*Alice and her mother were members of an elite underground group in Belgium. Hirsch is an engineer who works in data communication.*

105

*Aviva Blumberg (center) with her sister, Esther, and mother.*
(Credit: Museum of Jewish Heritage, New York)

# AVIVA BLUMBERG

POLAND

*"I decided that when the war ended, I'd never be Jewish again"*

In 1939, when I was eight and my sister, Esther, was thirteen, war broke out in Poland. Almost immediately the SS came to our apartment looking for my father, who was well known in Warsaw as a newspaper reporter and editor for the Jewish press. At the time my father was in Switzerland attending a Zionist conference. When he heard the news, he tried to get back to us but couldn't, so instead he made his way to the United States.

Over the next two years he sent letters to my mother through the Red Cross saying he was trying to get us visas to join him. Finally in 1941 he was successful, but by then it was too late for us to get out of Poland.

Already we had been forced to move into the Warsaw ghetto with thousands of other Jews. There we were assigned work in a factory, which temporarily protected us from being sent away. My job was collecting iron scraps from buildings no longer being used. Every morning I'd leave the ghetto with my work crew and come back at the end of the day. On the daily trips outside the ghetto I'd see Polish people selling newspapers and cigarettes.

107

In July 1942 the Germans started rounding up the ghetto workers, so my mother, sister, and I weren't safe anymore. My mother's friend said either we escape now or never. But my mother was afraid because she and Esther had dark hair and didn't look at all Polish. She was sure they would be captured. Even though I was blond and fair-skinned, my mother didn't want to let me go and kept me with her until the situation became very dangerous. Finally she told her friend to inquire whether any of the Polish women selling papers outside the ghetto might take me.

A very poor woman named Maria Rychowiecki agreed to hide me for money, which we didn't have. But with the help of the Jewish underground and a Polish man who didn't know me but had been a business partner of a family friend, we got enough together.

In preparing for my Polish life, the underground instructed me to tell people that I was Maria's niece on her side of the family, and that my parents had been killed in the war. I was to call her and her husband, Joseph, "Auntie" and "Uncle" in Polish. The underground also said I should pick a Polish name for myself. I chose *Jadwiga,* which sounded like Aviva, and *Jaworska,* which meant "tree."

Now that I was leaving the ghetto, I was excited. After having been closeted in for years, I couldn't wait to see the outside world. At the same time I felt awful separating from my mother and sister, although I was sure I'd be seeing them again.

In April 1943 we said good-bye. My mother had sewn my father's address in America inside my coat. Without telling her, because I knew it was very dangerous, I had taken three photos of the family.

That morning I left the ghetto with my work crew. Instead of returning with them at the end of the day, I took off my starred armband and went in the opposite direction with Wanda, the Rychowieckis' daughter, who like me was eleven and a half. I was scared. For years Jews had been allowed only to march in long lines down the middle of the street, and now we were on the sidewalk. I was waiting for someone to notice me and pull me away.

Nine days later the Warsaw ghetto went up in flames. As I watched it from the street, I hoped my mother and sister were safe. Right after that I started wetting my bed.

It took me a few weeks to settle in with the family. Their life was different from the way mine had been. They didn't have a bathroom or running water in their house. And there were no books around. Although they weren't religious— they seldom went to church—Maria taught me the Catholic prayers in case I was ever questioned.

When she was satisfied that I could pass as a Pole, she let me sell newspapers on the street as Wanda did. My route was around the ghetto walls. Every time I walked by, I felt terrible knowing my family wasn't there anymore.

From the beginning Maria and Joseph treated me like their own child and sometimes even better. They gave me a glass of milk each day because my mother had requested it, even though milk wasn't part of their normal diet and it was expensive. Since Joseph was sick with tuberculosis and couldn't work, the Rychowieckis had little money. The monthly payments they received for my keep made a big difference to them.

Besides the money, there was another reason they were risking their lives for me, and it wasn't because they loved

Jews. They were very nationalistic and hated the Germans for telling them what they could and could not do. Until Joseph got sick, he had been active in the Polish underground, working against the Germans.

Meanwhile I was masquerading as a Polish Christian. Yet I was always terrified. Every time I walked down the street, there were Germans mingling with the crowd. Sometimes a German soldier, trying to be friendly, would talk to me. One even lived near our house. Since he wasn't a storm trooper who rounded up Jews, I wasn't *that* afraid of him. Still, I always had to be on guard, especially because our next-door neighbor had the reputation of denouncing Jews. As soon as I moved in with the Rychowieckis, this neighbor started spreading the rumor that I was Jewish. When Joseph heard about it, he told the man I was his niece and if he tried to harm me his life would be in danger. After that the man left me alone.

Every now and then a cousin on Joseph's side visited us. From the start he noticed I wasn't like the other kids in the neighborhood, who had very little schooling. Although I had gone only as far as first grade, I knew a lot because books and music were part of my family's life.

This particular cousin played the violin, and when he came by I would sing the melody from Mozart's *Eine kleine Nachtmusik.* He was very impressed that I knew the piece and realized I stood out. He probably suspected I was Jewish, although Maria and Joseph never mentioned it.

A few months after I arrived, Joseph died, and from then on Maria started drinking a lot. Whenever she got drunk, Wanda and I were afraid she might blurt out my identity. Maria too was scared, because once she actually slipped and talked about my Jewishness. Luckily we were alone then.

Otherwise I felt very comfortable and safe with her. On Christmas, the first I ever celebrated, she made a wonderful dinner while Wanda and I decorated the tree. Maria made me feel I was in her family.

And Wanda was like my second sister. From the beginning she was nice to me. She never complained about my having to share her bed or that she was doing anything special for me. She was a good friend. In fact, we got along better than Esther and I did.

Esther and I competed for our parents' attention, but it wasn't like that with Wanda and me. We two were into things together. When Maria would get drunk, we'd conspire to take some of her money and use it to go to the movies or to rent bicycles.

Once Wanda and I came upon an empty house and looted what had been left behind. Ukrainians who were working for the Germans caught us and sent us to a detention camp. I was petrified that we'd be deported, but on our third day there some nuns unexpectedly came to gather children, and Wanda and I sneaked out with them.

Still, I couldn't get my sister and my mother off my mind. Every month when the woman from the underground brought Maria her money, I'd ask if she had heard about them. But she didn't know anything.

I kept wondering, Why is this happening to me? I didn't even come from a religious background, and yet I was suffering because I was Jewish. I decided that when the war ended, I'd never be Jewish again.

In August 1944 the Poles in Warsaw rose up against the

Germans and were defeated. As punishment, the Germans removed the Polish people to farms outside of the city. Maria and Wanda were sent to one farm and I to another. The farm family I stayed with didn't know I was Jewish. They were religious Catholics and made me go to church with them and kneel and say prayers before a small altar they kept in their house. I didn't want any religion and mumbled the prayers to get through them. But because being Jewish meant danger, I was determined to rid myself of that religion even more than Catholicism.

It was hard for me on the farm. I had always lived in the city, and now I was put in charge of huge cows. They terrified me. Even worse was being separated from Maria and Wanda. Although I saw them from time to time, I missed them a lot. They had become my family.

Finally in December 1944 the war ended in Poland, and we were back together again. We went to Warsaw, hoping to start our lives over. But after the Polish uprising, the Germans had demolished all the houses in our neighborhood. There was no place to live, and there were no jobs.

Maria and Wanda found work for me on another farm while they went to stay with relatives in the country. This time they were far away from me. I was so unhappy.

I had just turned thirteen and was making no attempt to find Jews who had survived the war and who might help me. Instead I continued to pass as a Pole, staying on the farm through the potato planting season even though the work was difficult. But I was very lonely.

On Sundays I'd walk for two hours to the village where Maria and Wanda were and visit with them for a little while. The rest of the week I was by myself. By April I realized how unhappy I was and decided to look for work in the town where Maria and Wanda were staying. I knocked on every door, asking people if they needed a housekeeper or a nanny. But nobody wanted my services.

Then one day Wanda heard about a Jewish family that had come back to the town, and she urged me to talk to them. Since I was too embarrassed to walk up to strangers and ask for help, she brought me to their house.

When the family opened the door, I said, "I am Jewish," and burst into tears. I told them who my father was and that he had been well known in Warsaw. The next day they took me to the city, which was about four hours away. There I met a family friend of ours who had been with the underground. He was happy to see me.

In the meantime my father had been bombarding the underground with letters, asking about his wife and children. They had not answered him because they had no information. Now they wrote to tell him I was alive. Until they heard from him, they didn't know what to do with me. So I was sent to a children's home, where I prepared for my high school entrance exam.

When my father finally located me, he started sending me letters and packages. One had a white bar of Swan soap. Everyone was very impressed.

In September 1945 my father made arrangements for me to go to Sweden to stay at the Polish embassy until my visa to the United States was ready. Before I left, Maria and Wanda came to the children's home to say good-bye. It was difficult parting from them but not as traumatic as it had been leaving my mother and sister in the ghetto.

I stayed in Sweden until November, and then on my

fourteenth birthday I boarded a ship for the United States. Ten days later I arrived there. I felt numb. It was as if I had been anesthetized and was walking through a haze.

My father didn't even recognize me—I had changed so much since I was eight. But I knew who he was and started crying. In Polish, I called him "Mr." instead of "Father." I hadn't used the word *father* in so long.

When my father realized who I was, he went wild. He hugged me so tightly, I was nearly black and blue. As the baby of the family, I was always special to him. And now I had survived the war.

### POSTSCRIPT

Almost as soon as I arrived in America, I began writing to Maria and Wanda, and they wrote back to me. When Wanda said she wanted to live in the United States, my father applied to get papers for her and said she could stay with us until she found a job.

Meanwhile I learned that Esther had died in the Warsaw ghetto uprising, and my mother had been in a concentration camp and had probably died there.

Suddenly, in 1947, before coming to America, Wanda contracted meningitis and died too. She was only seventeen. I felt as though I had lost another sister.

After that I still kept in touch with Maria, sending her letters and food and clothing. In 1961 I went to Poland and visited her. By then she was elderly and sick.

*Aviva in 1993.*

We talked a little about Wanda and about our lives today. And I thanked her for being so nice to me, especially mentioning the milk. I told her she was good person, but she didn't seem to think she had done anything special. Yet I know that because of her, Joseph, and Wanda I was given a second life. They're responsible for my being alive today and having my wonderful son, Richon.

*Aviva is a psychotherapist.*

115

*Ruth Bachner, age 7 $^1/_2$, with her mother and brother, Kurt.*

# Ruth Bachner

BELGIUM

## *"For me being safe was paradise"*

On the night of November 10, 1938, in Vienna, Austria, where I was born, the Germans suddenly smashed all the windows in my parents' clothing store. They sealed off the store and forbade my parents to enter it again. The next day I overheard my parents say that the same thing had happened to other Jewish shopkeepers and that all the synagogues had been vandalized too. Now German soldiers were dragging Jews into the street and taking them away on trucks.

I was eight at this time, and my brother, Kurt, was four. We didn't understand what was going on, but we sensed our parents' terror. I remember becoming especially frightened when the twenty-one-year-old janitor of our building came to our door dressed in a Nazi uniform and told us the apartment was now his.

After that we spent two months living with my uncle while my father arranged for us to get to Germany to be smuggled across the border into Belgium. Once there, we applied for papers to go to the United States. But before they came through, the Germans occupied Belgium and we couldn't get out.

117

By 1942, SS men were everywhere, rounding up Jews by the thousands. One Sunday as I was walking home, a neighbor from across the street whistled to get my attention and motioned for me not to go into my apartment. Terrified, I ran to my uncle's house, where I found my parents and brother. My parents told me that a Jewish informer had pointed out our apartment to the Nazis, and now we were no longer safe.

That's when they decided to send Kurt and me to live with a Gentile family who had a home in the suburbs. The family, the Belhommes, were already hiding a five-year-old Jewish girl.

When I heard I was getting out of the city, I was relieved, especially since my parents promised to visit every weekend. At the same time, I knew from notices the Germans had posted everywhere that the Belhommes could be arrested for hiding us.

Before my parents drove me to the Belhommes', they changed my name to a Christian one, Marie-Renée Leroi, and said I had to keep my religion a secret. I was very upset. I liked my name and I liked being Jewish. I didn't understand why this fact had to be hidden. Have I done something wrong? I wondered.

Kurt, who was only seven, was more confused. He hated being separated from our parents and made a scene when they left. After that he clung to me and wouldn't let me out of his sight.

The Belhommes had two children, Marcelle, who was Kurt's age, and Marguerite, who was eleven like me. Marguerite and I shared a room, and we went to school together. It wasn't long before we became best friends.

118

Marguerite was the only one I talked to about being Jewish. She'd say in a whisper, "That's our big secret," and I knew I could trust her.

But I wasn't sure about her mother. Although she included Kurt and me in everything the family did, she screamed and hit her children, and that scared me. Mr. Belhomme, who was easygoing, would say to me, "Don't mind Céline. She yells, but she doesn't mean it." Still, I was afraid that if I did something wrong she might have someone turn me in. So without complaining, I always cleaned my room and helped around the house.

Meanwhile, every Sunday for the next ten months, my parents came to visit. We went on picnics or stayed around the house. One weekend Mr. Belhomme suddenly told my parents that he could no longer keep my brother and me. He said it was getting too risky, and he was afraid he might get caught.

Now my parents quickly had to find another place to hide us. They had become friends with a Gentile woman in their apartment house who said that maybe Père Bruno, a priest she knew, could help. He found a convent that would take me in and an orphanage where Kurt could go. He also placed my parents with a wealthy family in the country who said they could work on their estate as domestics.

Before Père Bruno brought me to the convent, my father explained why I had to go there and what it might be like. I knew how important Judaism was to him and said, "Papa, I will always be Jewish. You don't have to worry about this."

But that wasn't uppermost in my father's mind. He was more concerned that I be safe. He took out three American one-hundred-dollar bills, which he had obtained illegally on the black market, and sewed them into the hemline of my coat along with the names and addresses of his sisters living in New York. "Child," he said, "if Mama and I don't make it through the war, you have money and a place to go." I burst into tears.

The convent was a school where rich farmers' daughters got a good education. All the classes were taught by novices in their twenties who were very nice. My favorite was Sister Marie-Thérèse. She was gentle and had a kind voice.

The older nuns scared me. From the start they wanted me to convert and kept insisting I take private catechism lessons and be baptized. They said that if I didn't, I would burn in an eternal hell. I had promised my father not to betray our religion and refused to give in. When I sat in church, I mouthed the prayers.

The nuns kept pressuring me to change my mind. Over and over they talked about blemishes on my soul, which frightened me. I thought if I didn't listen to them I might not survive, and finally agreed to do what they said.

Every day a nun taught me about Christianity, and as time went on I started believing in it. When I was ready to be baptized, I welcomed Catholicism.

But to convert me, the mother superior first needed my parents' permission and told me to write and ask them for it. I was so convinced about my decision, I had no guilt about the promise I had made to my father.

Père Bruno delivered my letter, and my father replied to the mother superior, "If this saves my child's life, then let it be done."

Now the nuns had to find godparents for me. A wealthy baron and baroness with two children of their own agreed to be at my baptism and look after me, knowing I was Jewish.

The minute I became a Catholic I pretty much put Judaism out of my mind. I didn't even know when the Jewish holidays came around anymore. I just wanted to stay in the convent. For the first time in years I felt protected. Now I wasn't afraid that every knock on the door meant a German was coming to take me away.

The only bad part was missing my parents. Except through the letters that Père Bruno brought back and forth, I had no contact with them. I knew they were alive, but I didn't know where they were hiding. I worried they might not make it through the war.

I also thought about my brother. He was such a young kid, only eight. I was sure he must be having a hard time being all by himself in the orphanage.

In the meantime I kept very busy with services and classes, spending afternoons and weekends playing ball or going sleigh riding. I liked the girls I lived with. They were very nice. But I never could completely relax with them. I was always afraid one might find out I was Jewish and denounce me. Even when I went to confession, I didn't tell the priest I was Jewish. The mother superior knew my background, but I kept a distance from her, too, afraid I might cross her the wrong way. I wasn't sure whom to trust.

I also kept my religion a secret from Sister Marie-Thérèse, although I felt very close to her. She might have suspected I was Jewish, but since she didn't let on, I wasn't going to bring it up. Yet at night when she'd come into my room to braid my hair, I would talk to her about every other subject that was troubling me.

One day I saw blood on my underwear, and I ran to her crying, "Sister, Sister, I'm dying." She took me aside and in a motherly way said, "You're just becoming a young lady. It's God's way of developing a human being." She was so special and comforting. I wanted to be exactly like her. I wanted to become a nun.

After I had been in the convent for a number of months, my coat became noticeably shorter on me and no longer met the convent regulations. One morning a nun came to get it so it could be lengthened.

In terror I closed the door of my room and quickly ripped out the money and addresses my father had sewn inside the lining. I hid everything in my cubby. When the coat came back later, I saw that there had been no need to go through all that trouble. The seamstress had just lengthened it by sewing a thick navy band across the bottom. Still I was glad I hadn't taken a chance.

When I had been in the convent for two years, I began to suspect there were other Jewish girls there. I noticed three girls who lived in a building on the premises and didn't mingle with us. At Christmas, when everyone went home for vacation and I was waiting for my godparents to come for me, I spoke to the oldest girl, who was my age. Even though I had been baptized, I was glad to be with another person who was going through the same thing I was.

She said that the other two girls were her sisters. Six months later she told me her mother had joined them at the convent. I envied her because she was with her family while I didn't know where my parents were. She said she was jealous of me because I went to classes and had fun with the girls while she spent the day being bored. Either way, we both felt safe in the convent. And for me being safe was paradise.

The convent had become my cocoon. I felt protected there and surrounded by good people. I never thought the Germans would come by, and soon I blocked out the war. My greatest worry was that my parents might not be alive.

One day in September, after I had been in the convent for a year and a half, Belgium was liberated. With bombs still flying, my mother suddenly arrived in a truck driven by Mr. Belhomme. When I saw her, I rushed into her arms and became hysterical. Then I noticed my father wasn't there and almost panicked. He was in Brussels getting the apartment ready for us, my mother told me.

"Now, Ruth, it's time to go home," she said.

But I refused to leave. I wanted to stay in the convent and become a nun. My mother was shocked. She kept saying, "Come home first and see Papa, and then you'll decide what to do."

So with a statue of the Virgin Mary under one arm and my prayer book under the other, I went with my mother and Mr. Belhomme. First we got Kurt, and then we rode back to our old apartment in Brussels.

As soon as I came into the house, I put the Virgin Mary on the mantelpiece, then I said hello to my father. Suddenly I remembered the three hundred-dollar bills in my coat. My father was amazed I still had the money. When I told him what I had done before the coat was lengthened, he said, "My Ruth. Such a smart girl."

That Sunday I got up early and woke Kurt. I told him to

*Ruth and her family in 1946.*

get dressed so we could go to church. My parents thought we were going for a walk. But the following Sunday my mother figured out what was happening and wouldn't let me leave the house. Instead I read my prayer book in bed under the covers.

Soon after that, while my mother was dusting the Virgin Mary, it "accidentally" fell off the mantel and broke into smithereens. By then I was starting to feel more comfortable with the Jewish religion and wasn't devastated.

In December the Germans tried to recapture Belgium and once again I was placed in the convent, this time with Kurt. Since it was Christmas vacation, the mother superior felt we'd be safe there.

But I was no longer happy in the convent. Sister Marie-Thérèse had become a full nun and was somewhere else. And after four months of living with my parents, I felt truly Jewish again. Luckily the war ended shortly thereafter.

We stayed in Belgium for the next two years, and during that time my family visited the Belhommes and I got to see Marguerite. More than once my parents explained that the Belhommes and the nuns had taken a tremendous risk hiding Kurt and me. Until then I hadn't thought much about it. I had been too busy concentrating on my own survival. As I got older, though, I began to realize that all these people were responsible for saving my life.

*Ruth in 1993.*

POSTSCRIPT

Twenty-five years ago the Belhommes moved to Canada, and until my parents died, the four of them corresponded. Five years ago my husband and I went to visit them, and I saw Marguerite for the first time in so long. The two of us couldn't stop crying.

After that I went back to Belgium with my family so I could show them what I had experienced as a child. I took them to the convent, and when I rang the bell a nun came out to greet us. I told her I had been hidden there during the war

126

and that my name then had been Marie—"-Renée Leroi," she finished my sentence. "Don't you recognize me? I used to braid your hair." It was Sister Marie-Thérèse. She was seventy-five years old. I couldn't believe it.

Sister told me that she and the other novices hadn't known till my mother came for me that I was Jewish. But she said that either way it would have made no difference. And I saw that having lived in the convent didn't make me any less of a Jew. I learned a lot about Catholicism that I probably never would have known to such a degree. More important, though, the nuns made me feel safe in a crazy world. Because of them, I'm alive today.

*Besides Ruth and Kurt, Père Bruno rescued hundreds of other Jewish children in Belgium.*

*Ruth is a bookkeeper.*

*Debora Biron, age 10, in 1946.*

# DEBORA BIRON

LITHUANIA

## *"I wanted my mother"*

For the first four and a half years of my life I lived in Kovno, Lithuania, where my father was a furrier. We were quite wealthy and owned a very large house with a big garden.

Then in the summer of 1941 the Germans entered the city, and suddenly my life turned around. We were forced to move from our beautiful home into a barbed-wired ghetto that had no indoor bathrooms.

In the ghetto the Germans appointed my father a policeman to keep order among the Jews and act as an agent between the Jewish community and the Nazis. Sometimes he was sent away to perform duties, and for days I wouldn't know where he was.

Meanwhile the Germans kept waking us up in the middle of the night, forcing everyone to line up outside in the freezing cold. I'd stand there, half asleep, watching people be hung for stealing food or trying to escape.

A year and a half later there were rumors that the Germans were planning to round up the children. Herman Lurie, a man my mother had become friends with, told her that some Jewish parents were placing their children with Gentiles who were willing to take them in. He said my parents should quickly make plans for me.

But my father said, "Absolutely not! If we leave the ghetto, we leave together." My mother didn't agree.

The next time my father was called away on duty, she told me I would be going somewhere. That very night, when the men from the work brigade returned through the ghetto gate, I and another girl who was almost seven walked among them in the opposite direction. When we were on the outside, a Lithuanian Catholic woman named Natasha met us. She was dressed in a black coat with a white flower, just as my mother had described.

Natasha said, "Come quickly!" and threw us into a hay wagon that was waiting on the side of the road. Just as she was climbing in next to the driver, a German policeman came up to her. "I know what you're up to," he said loudly. "You have exactly one minute to get out of here with the children, or I will shoot."

For the next three hours I lay under the hay until we reached a house on top of a hill where two other children and four grown-ups were staying. I immediately recognized one woman, a friend of Herman's from the ghetto.

Natasha said that this was a safe house and I'd be living here for a while. She told me I always had to speak in a whisper and could not go near the window.

Every two or three nights Natasha came by and took me for a walk. When I'd ask about my mother, she'd tell me she had seen her and that my mother would be joining me soon. Then she'd point out houses in the distance and say that other little girls like me were being hidden there, and that we were all going to be fine.

After I had been in the safe house for a month, Natasha told me I was going to be moving on. Now I would be living on a farm with a family named Karashka who had a daughter my age. Natasha promised to visit me there every week. When she said good-bye, I cried.

It was late when the wagon driver dropped me off at the Karashkas' house, but they were waiting up for me. They gave me a big bowl of hot cabbage soup and sat with me as I ate. The first thing they told me was that my name would now be Yanita Ushkaite and I was to say I was their cousin from the countryside whose mother was sick. Then they showed me to my room.

In the middle of the night I awoke with terrible stomach pains. For hours I sat alone in the bathroom, afraid to call for help. I didn't want to cause the family trouble, thinking they might get rid of me.

The next morning when Mrs. Karashka came to wake me, she saw that I had a fever. She put wet towels on my head and every few minutes came in to check how I was. I could tell she was a nice person.

And I liked her daughter, Gruzia. When I was well, I couldn't wait to run around outside and play with her. But the Karashkas told me that even though their farm was in an isolated area, strangers might come by, and they weren't sure who they could trust. So I had to stay indoors and be quiet, which meant no shouting or laughing aloud, while Gruzia and her parents could come and go as they pleased. I was unhappy. I tried to entertain myself by drawing and looking at the picture books Natasha brought for me, but I was lonely. I wanted my mother and kept wondering when she would come and take me away from this place.

At least I had Natasha, who in the beginning visited every week. At that time she would give the Karashkas some of my mother's jewelry and furs to sell so they'd have enough money to care for me. She also would read me letters that my mother had written and take my drawings back to her.

But after a while Natasha came less often, and I was very lonely. When Mrs. Karashka tucked me into bed, she talked softly to me and did whatever she could to make me feel part of her family. But still I was sad.

After I had been with the Karashkas for about four months, a woman suddenly dropped her daughter off and then left. This girl and I became good friends. I was relieved not to be the only Jewish child in the house, and I liked having company.

A month later Natasha told me my mother was on her way too, which meant that Natasha wouldn't be visiting any-more. She said she had to spend her time finding safe homes for other Jewish children. When she left, I couldn't stop crying. I loved her.

Finally one day my mother arrived. When I saw her, I couldn't believe my eyes. I was happy to have her with me.

The other girl's mother came too, and we four shared a room. Soon Herman joined us, and we were five. Mrs. Karashka washed everybody's laundry and cooked for all of us, while Mr. Karashka did the farming. Still, there was never enough food, so we mostly ate bread and cabbage soup.

With so many people living together, the house was al-ways in turmoil, especially when the other girl's mother left to pick up a sewing machine and never returned. No one knew what happened to her.

A few weeks later two elderly people showed up; they turned out to be the girl's grandparents. Every minute was a new event. It was confusing not knowing what would take place next.

In the meantime I kept asking my mother, "Why isn't Papa here?" She said, "As a policeman he has an important job and can't leave the ghetto." But she finally told me that the Germans had taken him away. She said that when the war was over we'd look for him. From then on I tried to blot my father from my mind. It was too painful to think about what might have happened to him. Besides, I was worried about my own life.

By now the Germans were everywhere. It got so dangerous, we could no longer live upstairs and instead moved into the cellar under the kitchen. But Herman thought that wasn't safe either and decided we should build a bunker next to the cellar, where the Germans were less likely to look. He and Mr. Karashka designed the room.

It was seven feet long and very narrow. To get in and out, they made a trap door that opened into the hallway. It had wooden planks on top that matched the flooring. Underneath it was insulated with blankets and cotton so it wouldn't sound hollow when someone walked on it.

For one week we all helped build the bunker, sleeping in the day and digging at night. Hour after hour we shoveled earth into bags which Mr. Karashka emptied onto his field. Finally the bunker was finished. It was tiny, dark, and uncomfortable. Although we each had a quilt and a wooden board to sleep on, the earthen floor was always damp, so our clothing and blankets smelled musty.

Because there was hardly any fresh air in the bunker, we

kept the trap door braced open with a forked stick. At night the adults took turns being on guard to alert us if there was trouble.

Once we moved into the bunker, the Karashkas said we could go upstairs only to use the bathroom. But since they had told people I was their cousin and had an excuse for my living with the family, they said I could also go up to the kitchen to get food for myself and the others. I was proud that they trusted me. And I was happy to get away from the cramped, smelly bunker, even if only for a little while.

I hated living so tightly together with grown-ups who were irritable and constantly arguing. They fought if someone snored too loud, and they fussed over who should sleep in which bed. It got so bad, they began to tell one another to leave.

The worst was when they started talking about what they thought was happening to the Jews. That scared me. All I wanted was to lie in my mother's arms and listen to her read to me by the kerosene lamp.

Soon the Russians were bombing our area, always in the middle of the night. There was shelling in the forest next to our house. I was terrified, but I never complained. I didn't want to cause any extra problems. Besides, I thought this was what life was supposed to be like.

By then the Germans were searching for men to send to labor camps, so Mr. Karashka moved into the bunker with us while Mrs. Karashka and Gruzia slept in the cellar under the kitchen to escape the bombing.

One hot summer night we all woke up to the sound of thumping on the floor above. I recognized that sound from the ghetto. It was the boots of German soldiers, and it meant something bad.

Herman, who had been on guard, heard it first and quickly started to close the trap door. With each step above, he carefully moved the forked stick a tiny bit, not wanting to grab it fast, or the door would have slammed shut. Each second the tramping upstairs came nearer. If the trap door didn't close soon, the soldiers would find us.

Suddenly the house was silent. The soldiers were standing right above us. A moment before, the trap door had closed.

''Who's down there?'' a soldier shouted.

''It's only my child and me,'' Mrs. Karashka called from the cellar under the kitchen.

''Where's your husband?'' he yelled.

''He's at the front,'' she said.

The soldier went downstairs and took a look for himself. None of us dared to breathe. When the soldier was satisfied with what he saw, he and the others left.

Afterward that's all we talked about. Over and over we relived what had happened. We couldn't believe we had survived to tell the story.

Now I could better understand how the Karashkas were protecting us. All along Natasha and my mother had told me what wonderful people they were, and although I liked them a lot, I didn't realize until that night how they were risking their lives for us.

We stayed in the bunker for one more month. Then in August 1944 Russian troops marched through our village, and the Germans were finally gone. When it seemed safe, we crawled out of the bunker. A few days later we said good-bye to the Karashkas. After being in their house for a year, I was so happy to leave it. I wanted to get as far away from that place as possible.

After that Herman, my mother, and I walked to Kovno, thinking we could go back to our beautiful home. But the Russians had confiscated it, so instead we moved into an apartment that we had to share with lots of other people.

For the next year Herman and my mother worked at small jobs while we waited to see if my father or any of our relatives had returned from the concentration camps. We never heard a word about any of them. It was as if my father had evaporated into thin air.

Herman thought that with so many concentration camps having been in Poland, we'd have a better chance of finding people in our family there. So we left for that country. Herman was reunited with his brother-in-law, two of his sisters, and his mother. But in my family only my mother and I survived the war.

Eventually Herman married my mother and adopted me. In 1947, when I was eleven, the three of us came to the United States, and I started the fifth grade in school. I never went back to Lithuania, and I never saw or spoke to Natasha or the Karashkas again. But my mother didn't let me forget them. She always talked about how marvelous they were to us. On Christmas when she sent the Karashkas gifts, I helped wrap them and made the family cards.

*Debora in 1993.*

POSTSCRIPT

Over the years my mother told me that Natasha, a teacher, had been part of an underground network to save Jews, especially children. And she confided that Mr. Karashka had been preparing for the priesthood but had decided to give it up to marry Mrs. Karashka. The two then made it their mission to help Jews.

My mother kept in touch with the Karashkas and knew they had two more children. Because they were poor, she sent them clothing and coffee, which was hard to get in their country. Years later, when the Russians vacated Lithuania and we got our house back, my mother gave our home there to the Karashkas to have for the rest of their lives. Mr. and Mrs. Karashka died five years ago, but their children are still living in the house today.

*Debora is a travel agent.*

*Simon Jeruchim (right) after the war with sister,
Alice, and brother, Michel.*

# SIMON JERUCHIM

FRANCE

## *"I wanted them to find me another hiding place"*

The first time I came face to face with a German soldier was in 1940, when I was ten and a half. The Germans had just invaded Paris, and my father, my older sister, Alice, and I were fleeing on bikes to the countryside. (My mother and younger brother, Michel, were joining us later.) Suddenly we came upon a huge crowd watching French soldiers retreat on horses while a unit of Germans in motorized tanks was coming down the road.

The Germans wore goggles, black leather jackets, and shiny high black boots. In their powerful mechanized equipment they looked like giants from outer space. At that moment I felt we had lost the war.

A year later, when things had quieted down, we returned to the outskirts of Paris, where we lived in a non-Jewish neighborhood. Since we weren't at all religious, I felt very comfortable there.

But by the end of 1941 the Germans started clamping down on the Jews, and I had to wear a yellow star on my black school apron that spotlighted who I was. For the first time I was dramatically aware that I was Jewish.

From then on little by little our rights were taken away. But we didn't realize how much danger we were in, because

139

the news was censored. Then on July 14, 1942, while family friends were visiting us with their sixteen-year-old son, Joseph, we heard rumors that the following day all Parisian Jews would be arrested. That night the eight of us stayed with my family's Gentile housekeeper, sleeping on the floor.

The next morning we found out that the French police had taken away all the Jewish families in our building and were returning for us. Now we had to find a place to hide.

Through contacts we were sent to the suburban home of a French couple named Monsieur and Madame Bonneau. They were in their forties and looked very aristocratic, especially the husband, who was tall and erect and had a well-trimmed beard. Compared with my family, they seemed cold and strict, and yet I trusted them because they were willing to risk helping Jews. I also liked their twenty-one-year-old daughter, Madeleine, who was very friendly.

The Bonneaus said that Joseph, Michel, and I were to go with Ernst, a man with slick hair and a mustache who was sitting quietly in a corner. Alice would be staying with a farm family. And plans were still being made for the adults.

When it was time to part, my mother became hysterical. She said to Madame Bonneau, ''If something happens to my husband and me, you must promise to look after my children and give them a good education.'' I was embarrassed that she was emotional in front of these reserved people. And I thought she was exaggerating the danger. Still, I was sad saying good-bye.

Ernst took us three boys by train a hundred miles away to his huge dilapidated house, where he lived with his two teenaged brothers, who stole bicycles and then sold the parts, which were in short supply.

Ernst too was involved in a shady business. He bought live steers, slaughtered them on his property, and then packaged and sold the meat at high prices on the black market. The only good part about staying with him was that we ate plenty of beef, which was a luxury.

As soon as we arrived, Ernst told me he didn't want the responsibility of caring for a five-year-old and had arranged to send Michel to live with another family. When the son came on a bike to take Michel with him, I was very upset but couldn't do anything about it. I had to go along with what I was told.

As it turned out, Michel wasn't that far away, so every few weeks I walked several miles to see him. The LeCleres, the family who were caring for him, were very nice. They had gotten Michel a little desk and new clothes and shoes. Michel, though, was very confused. He couldn't understand why he was living with these strangers.

Joseph and I weren't happy either. Joseph suspected Ernst of dealing with the Germans and kept telling me that if we didn't get away from the house soon we'd probably be denounced. I became so scared that whenever I was the lookout for Ernst and his men as they slaughtered the meat, I was sure the next truck or car coming up the road was Germans coming to take me away.

Finally, after three months of being with Ernst, I wrote to the Bonneaus, even though they had explicitly told me never to contact them. I told them I was frightened living with Ernst and wanted them to find me another hiding place.

A week or so later Madeleine came to get me—Joseph stayed on—and together we went by train back to her house outside of Paris. When her parents saw me, they were very angry that I had disobeyed them and said that all of us could have gotten into serious trouble. As it was, they were still looking for a safe place to hide my parents, and now they had to find another home for me.

This time I would be going to Normandy on the coast of France, not far from where my sister was hiding. Until then I had no idea where Alice was, and I got excited hearing we'd be near each other.

The Bonneaus arranged for a woman named Madame Monier to take me to my new home by train. When I arrived at my stop, I was met by Madame Huard, the woman whose farm I would be staying at. It was a bleak autumn day, and she was dressed in black and was sitting in a horse-drawn two-wheeled carriage. As she drove me through the tiny hamlet, I felt as though I was stepping into another world.

Madame Huard's husband was a prisoner in Germany, and she and her ten-year-old daughter lived in a one-room house. During the day the daughter went to school, and an eighteen-year-old hired boy took care of the horses and did the heavy work. My job was to bring the cows to pasture, churn the butter, and chop the wood.

From morning till night we all worked hard without a minute to rest. It was a tough life, and I hated it. The worst was the loneliness. Madame Huard and her daughter didn't talk much. And the hired boy, who slept in a shed with me, tried to push me around, especially when we were alone. It got so bad, I finally convinced Madame Huard to let me sleep in the main room where we all ate and where she and her daughter shared a bed.

The main room was cold and damp and had a dirt floor. After coming from a fashionable city like Paris, I found it difficult to adjust. Everything was so primitive. We had only a knife to eat with, and there was no electricity or running water, so we couldn't bathe or brush our teeth. Even sleeping was strange. Madame Huard put dough under my quilt to rise for the morning bread, so I had to lie on my side.

By now I had outgrown my shoes and replaced them with wooden clogs that were too big for me and were rough inside. I filled the toe part with straw to make them softer, but that made walking very difficult.

I was miserable. I'd sit by myself with the cows and cry and cry. The only time I was free was when the cows weren't roaming into other fields or being chased by dogs. Then I'd occupy myself by building bridges and dams across the streams, whittling wood with my penknife and tying sticks together with grass. In a few months I had my own Wall of China. But I wanted to be with people.

Every few weeks I visited my sister and saw that she was with a family who treated her as one of them. They had a daughter fifteen years old, Alice's age, and the two girls had become good friends. When I saw how well Alice was doing, I thought, Why can't I be with a nice family too?

After living with Madame Huard four months, I decided to write to the Bonneaus again to say I was unhappy and to ask them to hide me somewhere else.

A few weeks later Madame Monier came for me. She said the Bonneaus were furious that I had written and told me I was never to do that again. "You could have all of us killed," she scolded.

"Can I at least send a letter to my brother?" I begged. Madame Monier said no.

It was a hard time for me, especially since Madame Monier could tell me nothing about my parents. She didn't know where they were or if they were alive. I couldn't imagine things being worse.

Madame Monier took me to a hamlet not that far from the one I had left. Now I was to live in a one-room shack next to a church with a fifty-year-old widow named Madame Prim. Every morning and on Sundays we went to church. I knew right away that this was a religious community, and without anyone telling me to, I pretended to be Christian even though it made me feel like a runaway convict.

Naturally the villagers asked who I was, and I said that my father was a German prisoner and my mother had no money to care for me, so I was working for Madame Prim. Since it was common for poor and orphaned city kids to be sent to help farmers, they believed my story.

Within a month I was rattling off the prayers and enjoying being in church too. I was fascinated by the architecture, the sculptures, and the stained glass windows. I'd sit there and think, How did they build those columns? What's holding those arches together? I had always loved art, and now more than ever I wished I had paper and a pencil to draw with.

One day, after I had been with Madame Prim for a few months, an eight-year-old girl named Annette and her seven-year-old brother, Maurice, arrived. I sensed they were Jewish, and although they never said anything, I could tell they felt the same about me.

144

Now the shack was crowded, so we moved into a larger house down the road. There I found some pencils and paper, and whenever I could, I drew the room, the road, the countryside. Mostly, though, I was very busy helping Madame Prim, who had severe arthritis and was often in pain. When she was irritable, she hit Annette and Maurice, but I was spared because she depended on me to cook, bake, feed the rabbits, and take care of the garden. In season I also hired myself out to farmers to pick apples.

Life wasn't easy and I wasn't happy, but I knew better than to contact the Bonneaus again. Besides, Annette and Maurice had become attached to me and were relying on me as a big brother.

All this time I didn't know how the war was going. Without a radio or newspapers in the house, I was afraid the Germans would be around forever and I'd never get to see my parents again. I missed them a lot, and I was worried about them.

Then suddenly I developed a severe rash all over my body—probably from not washing and not eating the right food. Madame Prim sent me to a hospital ten miles away that was run by nuns. The minute I got there, they stripped me naked and put me in a tub. It was my first bath in two years.

As the nuns scrubbed my body, they noticed I was circumcised. But they didn't say anything. They just bandaged me up and told me I had to lie still. For the next two weeks I had nothing to do but think about my parents. I realized that it had been years since I heard from them.

By then the Germans were all over the place, searching house to house for men to send to labor camps. From the hill where our farm was, I had seen them on the road, traveling in trucks and in armored cars. Luckily they had never come near our house.

But one day after I had recovered, I saw a German officer on a motorcycle driving at top speed in our direction. Instinctively I ran out the back door to alert the twenty-year-old son of the family next door. He quickly hid in a hayloft, and the Germans didn't find him.

After that Allied airplanes frequently flew overhead in the direction of Germany. From the shortwave radios some farmers had, word spread that the Allies were pushing the Germans out of France. As airplanes rained bombs on the next town, German soldiers frantically ran through our fields trying to escape.

I was terrified seeing them so close. After surviving the war this long, I was afraid the Germans would now find me. Madame Prim was scared too and said we should all hide in the attic. We stayed there for days and only came out when it seemed safe.

In July 1944 France was liberated and the war was over in that country. The first thing I did was write to the Bonneaus, asking if I could come back to Paris. Without waiting for an answer, I went to my sister's farm, took her bike, and pedaled two hundred fifty miles to the Bonneaus' house. They were surprised to see me, but this time they weren't angry.

The first question I asked was whether they had heard anything about my parents. From their expressions I knew something was wrong. They said that while Joseph's and my parents were trying to flee through the French countryside, they were denounced and arrested by the Germans. After that no one knew what had happened. Most likely they were

146

sent to a concentration camp, they said. I was in shock. It was a nightmare come true.

For the next year I stayed with the Bonneaus, and Alice came too, but Michel continued to live with the LeCleres. By then I was almost sixteen and resented Mr. Bonneau's strict rules. Still, I was always obedient. I was tired of being shipped from place to place and wanted the Bonneaus to keep me.

Then one day my mother's brother appeared at the door and said, "I'm your uncle." I didn't know who he was. Our families hadn't visited together much. He said that he felt it was his duty to take care of his sister's three children, and we were to go with him.

I didn't want to leave the Bonneaus and felt sick inside. I was finally blending in with their way of life—I had even joined the Protestant Boy Scouts—and now I was being uprooted again.

Michel was more confused. In one day he was whisked from the LeCleres and handed over to strangers. He didn't even know who I was and kept addressing me as "Monsieur."

As it turned out, we stayed with our uncle for only a short time. His apartment was too small for us and his own family, and he didn't have much money. So he sent us to a home for orphaned Jewish kids. There I learned about my religion and was one of the first French Jewish kids to be Bar Mitzvahed after the war.

We stayed in the orphanage for four and a half years until family members in the United States sponsored us to come to America. One of these relatives was my grandmother on my mother's side, who had left Europe in the thirties. By then I was nineteen and a half and had just finished my training in art school. Before I left France, I hitched a ride to Madame Prim's home to say good-bye to her, but neighbors told me I had come too late. Shortly after the war ended, she had died.

I then went to the hospital where the nuns had nursed me. I wanted to see it again so I could remember what it looked like. A drawing I had made of a nun was still hanging on the wall. The mother superior had put it there while I was a patient.

At this time I learned through Madeleine that her parents had died. I was sorry I had never gotten the chance to thank them for what they had done and to ask them why they had risked their lives for me. During my years in hiding I took them for granted and knew I could always count on them. Now that I was older, I realized I had survived the war because of them.

POSTSCRIPT

Four years ago my wife, Cécile, and I went to France and visited the little town where I had lived with Madame Prim. I didn't recognize any of the people, but the shack was still standing and so was the tiny church.

After talking to Joseph, who had escaped before the Gestapo came to arrest Ernst, I learned that Ernst, the LeCleres, Madame Monier, and the Bonneaus were all connected to the underground, with the Bonneaus overseeing everything.

148

*Simon Jeruchim in 1993.*

Now that I'm an adult, I've thought more about the Bonneaus and I realize they were wonderful people. It's amazing how much they put up with me during the war. Then afterward, they kept their promise to my mother and were willing to raise Alice and me. I'm deeply thankful to them. Because of what they did, I am alive today.

*Simon keeps in touch with Madeleine and the families who hid Alice and Michel. Recently he got a letter from Annette, who then visited with him and talked about her past. Simon is an award-winning package designer. He also paints, sculpts, and illustrates books.*

149

*Judith Steel, age 5, in 1943, with Maman Suzy.*

# JUDITH STEEL

*"They made me feel safe and wanted"*

I've been told by relatives that in 1939, when I was fourteen months old, my parents, my grandfather, and I sailed for Cuba on the S.S. *St. Louis*. We were 4 of 936 Jews trying to escape from Germany before it was too late. Unbeknownst to us, the Cuban government had already notified the Germans that we could not enter their country. And the United States also refused to take us in.

When the ship returned to Europe, Jewish organizations paid England, France, Holland, and Belgium to accept a number of the people. My family went to a small town in southern France, where we rented an apartment in a little house. Others had no place to go and ended up back in Germany, where they were eventually sent to the camps.

At that time it was still safe for Jews in France, so we didn't hide our religion. At home we spoke German, but soon I learned French from Suzy, our landlord's daughter. She was four years older than I, and we played a lot together. I particularly loved going to her house because her mother was affectionate and gave me attention. I called her "Maman Suzy," which I thought meant "Suzy's mother" in French.

In 1942 the situation for Jews in France became so dan-

151

gerous, my parents were afraid to leave the house. Maman Suzy would bring us chicken, milk, or potatoes from her friend's farm, but usually we went hungry.

My parents especially encouraged me then to visit Maman Suzy because she fed me. I'd stand outside her window and yell, "Maman Suzy, would you like me to come?"

She'd call out, "Yes, my little one. Come!"

One morning there was a loud knock on our door. It was the French police with orders to arrest my family. They put my parents and me on a truck and took us to Gurs, a camp where we were handed over to the Nazis. My grandfather, who was very sick in bed, was left behind.

For the next three weeks my mother and I lived in a crowded barrack while my father was somewhere else. One day my mother hugged me tightly and said, "You may never see Mommy and Daddy again." I could tell from her eyes that something was very wrong.

That night my father took me outside of the camp and brought me to a small room where there were a few other children. He pointed to a man who was holding out a drink and said, "Look at that." When I reached for the cup he let go of my hand. A second later he was gone. I started screaming.

The next morning Maman Suzy's husband, Josef, came for me. He said we were going to his house, where my grandfather was now living.

As soon as I saw Maman Suzy, I ran into her arms and cried. But she looked at me horrified. I had sores all over my body. Maman Suzy laid me across her lap and covered me with iodine. When that didn't help, she called the doctor. He knew I was Jewish but still came to the house to treat me. As he was leaving, I overheard him tell Maman Suzy I was in such bad condition from not eating that within a few weeks I would have died.

When I recovered, Maman Suzy said, "From now on, I'm going to be your mother." She was pregnant at the time and told me I'd be brought up just like one of her own children. Then she changed my last name to hers, Enard. After that, I was part of the family. Instead of calling her "Maman Suzy," I now called her "Maman," and Josef "Papa."

Both Maman and Papa treated me well, but I always felt closer to her. When she sang French songs, I was sure they were meant for me. A few months later Jacques was born. I considered him my brother and Suzy my sister.

Meanwhile my grandfather had a stroke and went to the hospital. I visited him there just once, and after that I never saw him again.

Now the only family I knew was Maman's, and I felt a part of it. I liked playing with the animals around the house and stood and watched Papa when he slaughtered pigs. I even ate the snails Maman cooked. And on Sundays I went to church with the family, singing the hymns and making the sign of the Cross.

That September I started kindergarten. Suzy and I told everybody at school we were sisters, and they believed us.

Meanwhile Maman told Suzy and me she was hiding an old Jewish artist named Lazarre in the attic. Whenever I'd go up there to get toys, I'd see him, but we rarely talked.

Soon it was summer, and Maman wanted to send me to the day camp that Suzy had been going to. It was run by nuns, but not those from the church we attended. On the day it started, Suzy and I walked there together. The priest didn't recognize me and asked Suzy who I was. She said I was the Jewish girl her parents were taking care of. When he heard that, the priest said he couldn't accept me because I would put the other children in danger. So that summer both Suzy and I stayed home.

Even though many of the people in town remembered I was Jewish from the time I had lived with my parents, Maman kept warning me to be careful. She said these people probably wouldn't turn me in, but if the wrong person found out, we all could be killed. She told me I had to keep quiet about my past. The only time I felt open and free was with the family. They made me feel safe and wanted.

Still, I was hoping my parents would come back for me, and often asked Maman when that day would be. She'd say, "In time, my child. Right now this is your home." And I accepted it. I felt so comfortable, I soon forgot a war was going on.

But one day in 1944, while Suzy and I were out wheeling Jacques in his carriage, we heard gunshots coming from the center of town. Suddenly people started running in all directions. Suzy and I grabbed Jacques and raced into a jewelry store, where we stayed until it got quiet.

The next day German soldiers arrived at our house and took over Papa's furniture factory, which was connected to where we lived. They said that now Papa had to work for them.

Since I had a slight German accent, Maman was terrified. She worried that the soldiers might wonder why a German child was living with a French family. "If they realize you are Jewish, we'll all be dead,'' she said. She warned me not to speak when the soldiers were nearby.

I listened to what Maman said, and when the soldiers were around, I stood there and smiled without saying a word. At first it was like a game, but when I noticed their guns, I shook inside.

Sometimes I understood what the soldiers were saying. One said in German that I was pretty and looked just like Maman. Later I said to Maman, "See, I *am* your child."

Meanwhile I was still going to school and playing outdoors to make everything appear normal. But the longer the soldiers were in the town, the more nervous Maman and Papa became. Maman suddenly decided I looked Jewish because my ears stuck out too much. She decided to cover them by pulling my hair tightly over the tops, and she combed Suzy's hair the same way. She practically dressed Suzy and me alike, too. Having the same coloring as Maman, we sort of resembled each other, which Maman hoped made me less noticeable to the Germans.

One night from my bedroom I overheard Maman and Papa talking about the camps and saying they thought my father had died. Since they didn't mention my mother, I asked Maman the next morning when she would be coming back. Maman didn't give me a definite answer, so I expected my mother to arrive on my birthday, which was in February.

At the end of August 1944 the Germans who had been around our house for a few months suddenly told us they were leaving and said good-bye. Right after that France was liberated. Two days later Maman said that Lazarre had gone too, as had the four other Jews who had been hiding in the attic. I hadn't even known they were there.

Now that the war was over, I started thinking more about my mother and kept waiting for her to come. But it didn't happen. So for the next year and a half, I stayed with Maman, believing, This is where I'll live forever. Then one day she told me I was going to the United States to live with my aunt and uncle. She said that they were rich people and would give me a good life.

I was crushed. Here I had no parents, and now I was being taken away from Maman. I loved her, and I knew she loved me. She was always kind and protected me. I begged to stay with her, but she said it was impossible.

Maman took me to a Jewish organization in Paris that was temporarily caring for sixty-eight children whose papers were being made ready for passage to America. The few weeks I was there, Maman visited. Right before I left for America she came to say good-bye. When she hugged and kissed me, I couldn't stop screaming, I was so frightened.

After ten days on the seas the ship docked, and I was met by my aunt and uncle and their two sons. I felt totally lost. I didn't know who they were, and I couldn't speak English, their language.

It was hard for me, and for them too. The first year I only wanted to be with Maman. I missed her so much. But as time went on, I got used to my new family and felt at home with them.

For years and years I didn't contact Maman, and she didn't get in touch with me. But she was still on my mind. She had been special. I never forgot her.

156

*Judith and Maman in 1992.*

### POSTSCRIPT

Last year, after attending an international conference for hidden children in New York, I decided to visit Maman. She was now seventy-nine, and I was afraid that if I didn't see her soon it might be too late.

I got her telephone number from Suzy's daughter, Patricia, who lives in the United States, and one day I finally made the call. In French I told her who it was and said, "Maman, should I come?" She answered, *"Oui, oui."*

157

A month later I flew to France and spent a week with Maman. We hadn't been together in forty-six years, but it was as if we had seen each other an hour ago.

She and Papa were divorced. When I asked her why they risked their lives to hide six Jews, she said, "It was the thing to do." Maman's friend who had the farm where she got the chickens and milk for my family hid seven people in her hayloft.

*Judith in 1993.*

"Anyway," Maman said, "how could I not take you in? You were so little." She didn't have to say, "It was because I loved you." I knew that all the time.

Now we phone each other every few weeks. When I call I say, "I just wanted to hear your voice." Maman has been like a mother to me. I thank God I've had her in my life.

*In June 1993 Maman received a medal and a certificate from Yad Vashem Museum in Jerusalem for saving the lives of six people. Judith and Patricia went to France to be with her when she was given this honor. Judith is an electrologist.*

# ACKNOWLEDGMENTS

Many people have helped me with this project and I wish to thank them: Esther Brumberg, Research Coordinator of the Museum of Jewish Heritage, for referring numbers of people whose stories appear in this book; Rabbi Daniel Isaak, for taking time from his busy schedule to assist me; Helina Masri and Ann Shore of The Hidden Child Foundation of the Anti-Defamation League, for returning my numerous phone calls and leading me to the right sources. I am also grateful to those people who called their co-workers, congregants, friends, and family members, encouraging them to share their stories with me.

Most of all, my thanks and appreciation go to the now-adult men and women who trusted me with their personal histories. Some of them had never before confided the painful details of their past, yet they agreed to talk to me so that their grandchildren and future generations could learn what had happened years back, when the world was in havoc.

Although I did not meet any of the rescuers, I owe them profound thanks. If not for their extreme bravery, the stories in this book could not have been told. ''By saving one life, they are as one who has saved an entire world'' (The Talmud).

# GLOSSARY

**Anti-Semitism:** Having or showing prejudice against Jews

**Aryan:** Word used by Nazis to mean "caucasian of non-Jewish descent"

**Auschwitz:** Site of the Nazi concentration camp in SW Poland where masses of people were exterminated

**Black market:** Selling goods illegally

**Ghetto:** Section of city where Jews were forced to stay

**Hasidic:** Referring to a pious Jewish sect originating in Poland whose members joyfully worship God

**Holocaust:** Systematic destruction of over 6 million Jews by the Nazis

**Messiah:** In Judaism, the promised deliverer of the Jews

**Psalms:** Sacred songs and poems

**Reich:** German government

**Shabbat:** The Jewish sabbath

**Shul:** Synagogue

**Tallit:** Prayer shawl

**Torah:** Jewish religious literature, laws, and sacred writings

**Underground:** Groups organized in strict secrecy during World War II in Nazi-occupied countries to resist the German invaders. In France the underground was known as the Maquis.

# FURTHER READING

CHAIKIN, MIRIAM. *A Nightmare in History: The Holocaust 1933–1945*. New York: Clarion Books, 1987.

GREENFELD, HOWARD. *Hidden Children*. New York: Ticknor & Fields Books for Young Readers, 1933.

LANDAU, ELAINE. *We Survived the Holocaust*. New York: Franklin Watts, 1991.

MELTZER, MILTON. *Rescue: The Story of How Gentiles Saved Jews in the Holocaust*. New York: Harper & Row, 1988.

ROGASKY, BARBARA. *Smoke and Ashes: The Story of the Holocaust*. New York: Holiday House, 1988.

ROTH-HANO, RENÉE. *Touch Wood: A Girlhood in Occupied France*. New York: Four Winds Press, 1988.

TEC, NECHAMA. *Dry Tears*. Connecticut: Wildcat Press Company, Inc., 1982.

TOLL, NELLY. *Behind the Secret Window*. New York: Dial Books, 1993.

VAN DER ROL, RUUD and RIAN VERHOEVEN FOR THE ANNE FRANK HOUSE. *Anne Frank: Beyond the Diary, A Photographic Remembrance*. New York: Viking, 1993.